# LIVES&
## LEGACIES

# Maimonides

SERIES EDITOR: BARBARA LEAH ELLIS

# ILIL ARBEL

# Maimonides

## A Spiritual Biography

*A Crossroad 8th Avenue Book*
The Crossroad Publishing Company
New York

BP 53

The Crossroad Publishing Company
481 Eighth Avenue, Suite 1550
New York, NY 10001

First published in 2001 by The Crossroad Publishing Company

LIBRARY OF CONGRESS CATALOGING-IN-PUBLICATION DATA
Arbel, Ilil
Maimonides : a spiritual biography / by Ilil Arbel.
p. cm.   (Lives & Legacies)
Includes bibliographical references and index.
ISBN 0-8245-2359-8 (hardcover)
1. Maimonides, Moses, 1135-1204.   2. Rabbis—Egypt—Biography.
3. Jewish philosophers—Egypt—Biography.
I. Title.

BM755.M6 A78        2001
296.1'81—dc21
[B]        2001002817

Printed in the United States of America
Set in Janson
Designed and produced by SCRIBES Editorial
Cover design by Kaeser and Wilson Design Ltd.

1  2  3  4  5  6  7  8  9  10  04  03  02  01

5/25/06

*To the memory of my parents, Ida Wisotzky-Rosenfeld and Dr. Leibek (Arieh) Rosenfeld, and to their home that overlooked Rambam Street*

# CONTENTS

# Maimonides

מעשה ברבי מיימון זלה״ה

The bronze statue of Maimonides at Plaza of Tiberiades, near the synagogue in Córdoba, Spain. (Photo by Gregory Frux)

# 1

## Sunrise in Andalusia

From the rising of the sun to its setting, from north to south, there never was such a chosen people [as the Jews of Spain] in beauty and pleasantness, and afterwards, there will never be another such people.

—*Isaac Abrabanel*

"I AM NOTHING but dust and ashes."

Rabbi Maimon ben Joseph may have found solace in Abraham's ancient words as the young woman was lowered into her grave. The legends tell she was a butcher's daughter, and that the community disapproved of the marriage between them. A rabbi must marry a scholar's daughter who would know how to run his household, declared the Talmud, and Rabbi Maimon represented the eighth generation of leaders in the Jewish community of Córdoba. He served as a *dayyan*, a judge of the rabbinical court, a man of great consequence in his middle years. She must have been a special person, that young woman whose name has been lost to us, because Rabbi Maimon loved her so much he had to marry her anyway. And so he had a dream-vision, and in the dream God commanded him to marry the butcher's daughter; the community respected prophetic dreams and accepted the unsuitable marriage.

Rabbi Maimon and his wife shared only one precious year of happiness, and then she died in childbirth; the tight-knit community sadly gathered in the Jewish cemetery to say goodbye. Not very far off, her newborn child slept, his large dark eyes shut against the world, blissfully unaware of the genius he inherited from this unlikely union, and of the extraordinary future that awaited him.

He would grow to be the greatest Jewish philosopher and Talmudist of all times. Eight hundred years after his death, his work is as vibrant and pertinent to our lives as it had been during his lifetime. Moses Maimonides was to influence Jewish and non-Jewish philosophers alike, with such diverse individuals as Spinoza, Leibniz and Thomas Aquinas freely acknowledging their debt to him. Yet the intelligent layman can understand and relate to his work with ease; his rigorous thinking translates into elegant writing that is simple and direct, visceral as well as intellectual. His book, *The Guide of the Perplexed*, is one of the most influential philosophical works of any time.

If the image of a staid, respectable clerical gentleman comes to mind when the name of Maimonides is mentioned, dismiss the thought. His life was a roller coaster of dismal persecution and dazzling success, touched by personal and professional controversy that has never quite settled. It took him from the plight of a persecuted refugee in his own land, to the Arabian Nights' splendor of a sultan's court and harem. Maimonides was described as an adventurer, a leader, a philosopher, a Talmudic scholar, a correspondent, a writer, a rationalist, a scientist, a doctor, a man of the law, a tormented soul and a prophet driven by his own image of God. A complicated figure against a fascinating historical background, he was all of these, and more.

MOSES BEN MAIMON, KNOWN in Hebrew literature as the *Rambam* and in Western culture since the Renaissance by the Greek *Maimonides*, was born at one o'clock in the afternoon of March 30, 1135, into an era of splendor. Spain, under Islamic rule, was enjoying a true "Golden Age," and the Jews, more than during any other time in history until the twentieth century, fully participated in it. They took part in politics, culture, science, medicine and commerce. Córdoba, a city of legendary beauty and sophistication, was home to many ethnic groups and cultures, together creating a rich, exciting atmosphere. Some Arab geographers claim that almost half a million people resided in the city and the suburbs surrounding it, though the real number could have been anything between that and a hundred thousand. Even the low estimate is quite large for any city at that time. Córdoba had hundreds of mosques, thousands of public baths, and numerous well-stocked libraries and observatories. Schools flourished and well-equipped hospitals served as centers for the study of medicine. As part of Islamic Spain, Córdoba accorded its citizens full religious freedom. Regarding Jewish studies, Córdoba slowly replaced the Babylonian cities of Sora and Pumbaditha as the center of Jewish learning. Strolling among the sparkling fountains and tiled pools, relaxing in the well-tended gardens, the inhabitants and the many visitors enjoyed paved streets, illumination in most public areas and in many private homes, even indoor plumbing. As a center of industry and commerce, the city granted good employment to all who needed it, at all levels of education, and extraordinary luxuries to those who could afford them.

Trade was the core of Islamic economy, and included much travel, both on land and sea. Muslims viewed travel for the sake of learning as even more important than for commerce, as it was highly recommended in the Koran. Jews felt similarly—traveling for the purpose of learning was also highly regarded by the Talmud. However, they also traveled for commerce, political reasons and for creating marriage alliances with Jewish families overseas. Generally, Jews preferred sea voyages because traveling by ship did not desecrate the Sabbath, but during winter they had to travel by land caravans. Land travel was more expensive because the caravan had to stop for a full day every Sabbath. A wealthy Jew often owned houses in three different countries, and credit was established between commercial families, facilitating all forms of trade. Christians, Muslims and Jews traded freely with one another, sharing a truly cosmopolitan society. Correspondence and travel books from this era, such as the Arabic *Book of Roads and Kingdoms* and the Jewish book *The Itinerary of Benjamin of Tudela*, show how ordinary and even common such distant travel was, despite dangers from weather, pirates, robbers and local wars.

Such extensive commercial travel allowed constant intellectual exchange among the Jewish communities. Hebrew was their common language, so letters from various rabbis in distant lands could resolve matters of law and ritual. A commercial traveler often carried such letters with him. Rabbi's Maimon's correspondence, or responsa, as these letters were called, were eagerly awaited in many communities.

The location of young Moses' childhood home is debated. Most likely he was born in the *Judería*, the Jewish quarter. No stigma was attached to living in this section. Jews preferred to live in concentrated neighborhoods, where they could exercise mutual protection, but they experienced no restrictions or any form of segregation. Christians and Muslims also lived in groups, for the same reason.

At the wealthier parts of the Judería, each house was usually built around a central courtyard decorated with fountains, pools and stone columns. Ornamental and fruit trees flourished, ground covers and flowers draped the stonework, growing luxuriously and supplying coolness and beauty. Despite the traditional Jewish objection to any visual images that may suggest idolatry, some luxury homes belonging to courtiers even contained statues of animals such as lions and deer, showing how strongly the three cultures intermingled.

A Jewish household of a wealthy man like Rabbi Maimon was comfortable, well-furnished and afforded excellent food, including such luxury items as good wines, exotic fruit and costly spices. Valuable carpets from Egypt and Persia covered the stone floors, wall hangings and tapestries decorated the walls and beautiful textiles were purchased for household use and clothes. The rooms were filled with bowls of lead crystal, ivory carvings and beautiful ceramics—some produced locally, some imported. The lady of the house, and often the man too, wore clothing made of colorful silks, accessories of fine leather and precious jewelry. Private libraries included not only traditional Jewish texts, but extensive collections of works of philosophy, medicine and science and many works of ancient and contemporary poetry. Books were widely available, as paper was introduced into the Islamic world in the ninth century, by Chinese traveling merchants.

YOUNG MOSES WAS REARED in a household of love and a love of learning. Rabbi Maimon was a gentle, kind father, who fully understood and appreciated his son's intellect and special gifts. Undoubtedly, various nurses and servants helped raise the infant at first, but soon Rabbi Maimon was persuaded to marry again, as was the custom. We do not know much about his second wife, not even her name or any details about her lineage, but some facts can be deduced. No oral traditions point to any difficulties regarding Rabbi Maimon's second marriage, so we may assume she came from his own social strata, probably the daughter of one of the great Jewish families of Spain. When she gave birth to her own child, David, Moses loved his new brother with a profound, unconditional love that lasted a lifetime. Later, he spoke of David as his greatest joy in life. There was no jealousy in the child Moses' heart, no feeling of being apart or different. Much credit can be probably given to the stepmother for fostering such an atmosphere of love and joy.

Rabbi Maimon educated his sons at home. We know that from Maimonides himself, who claims, "First reading I learned from my father and teacher, may his memory be blessed, who learned it from his own rabbi." This was the custom, and Rabbi Maimon was well-suited to the task. Rabbi Maimon was a devoted and learned scholar, with a particular interest in astronomy and math, and a wide knowledge of Jewish law. He was the disciple of Joseph ibn Migash (1077–1141), who was himself a student of Alfassi and later succeeded him as the head of the school of Lucena; Rabbi Joseph was universally considered the greatest legal scholar in Spain. Rabbi Maimon wrote commentaries to the Talmud, a work on ritual and expository notes on the Pentateuch. He was an emotional, kind man, with a love of religion that was very different from that of his son Moses.

Rabbi Maimon saw God as a personal, loving entity, not as an intellectual abstraction. He loved the legends of the Aggadah (the metaphorical, non-legal sections of the Talmud), believed in angels and wrote with deep and poetic emotion, with many images and allegories. His Letter of Consolation, written in response to an inquiry or request for guidance by a perplexed and despairing community of Jews, comforted many people with its innate kindness and sincere love for his fellow Jews. This simple faith supported Maimon during the years of wandering and trouble that were to come all too soon. His acceptance and submission to God's will acted as an example and comfort to the young and confused Moses, suddenly torn from his lovely home, tight-knit community and good prospects for the future and, often in fear for his very life.

Without Rabbi Maimon, it is unlikely that Moses could have developed, under such circumstances, his feeling of being "perfect with God," which meant so much to him throughout his life. His lifelong attempt to cultivate gentleness, modesty and even temper, succeeded despite his deep-seated knowledge of his superior intellect, social standing, lineage and a natural inclination to pride and dignity. These qualities might have developed into arrogance without the help of his father's gentle teaching.

In addition to his home studies, Moses spent some time with his father's old tutor, Rabbi Joseph ibn Migash, further enhancing his extensive education. Young Moses studied a curriculum that would astonish modern educators, but was not unusual for the time. Any well-educated Jew was well versed in astrology, astronomy, mathematics, geometry, science, optics, philosophy, calligraphy, law and rhetoric. Often he would be a linguist, capable of complicated translations in various languages; his knowledge of Arabic and Hebrew would be so extensive, he could compose poetry in both—and many were truly fine poets. Some of the greatest names in Hebrew poetry come from this era— Judah Halevi, Solomon ibn Gabirol, Abraham ibn Ezra. However, these poets regarded Jewish education as the most important part of their studies: the Bible, Mishna, Talmud, codes, commentaries. Later, when describing his education, Moses confessed to studying his father's medical books, probably on the sly. (One wonders if the indulgent Rabbi Maimon secretly knew that his precocious boy already showed interest in poisons, herbs and surgery.) One subject he did not like very much was poetry. Despite the immense popularity of the subject in the Islamic courts, and the prolific, excellent Jewish poetry produced at that time, Moses never had the capacity to express his feelings with the emotional surrender and sense of imagery needed for poetry, and stayed with the precision of prose. This deaf ear to poetry must have caused some frustration to Rabbi Maimon and Rabbi Joseph, but perhaps it accounts for his flawless, meticulous prose style and love of rationalism.

Legends abound in regard to Maimonides' early studies. Various story cycles, meant to represent Maimonides in almost superhuman ways, described him as ignorant and hard of learning as a child. Then by sheer magic—sometimes a kiss from a great rabbi, sometimes a blessing from Elijah the prophet—he suddenly acquired supernatural, profound wisdom. Legends of this type are typical and accompany the life story of many great leaders. Some of the oral traditions, however, contain elements of truth; those legends that tell about his apprenticeship under Rabbi Maimon and then a trip to Rabbi Joseph ibn Migash ring true, even when embellished with supernatural phenomena. And it is true that the young Moses at an early age astonished his teachers by his remarkable depth and versatility.

A subject Moses Maimon was profoundly interested in was his own genealogy, which left a lasting impression on the imaginative boy. The family took its lineage very seriously, and from the earliest age he had heard that he was a direct descendant of Rabbi Judah ha-Nasi, and that his line went further back through the royal house to King David himself. Rabbi Judah ha-Nasi was one of the greatest names in rabbinic Judaism, a second-century scholar and the editor of one of the most important legal texts of Judaism, the Mishna. King David was the most powerful and beloved ruler in the history of the Jews. The Messiah, for whom Jews are still waiting, is to be borne of this line. Such heritage is not a light psychological burden for a child; a strong sense of responsibility and an obligation to follow in the footsteps of such individuals was awakened in Moses. This lineage created a core of pride that no later humiliation in the hands of his persecutors, or his own aspiration to perfect humility, could ever erase. He also developed a strong relationship to the biblical Moses. Born on Passover Eve, it is possible that young Moses was at least partially named after that towering figure, so prominent in the Passover story, and for his entire life he considered the biblical Moses the greatest of the prophets and his spiritual mentor. Later, a Jewish saying would declare: "From Moses to Moses there were none like Moses."

And suddenly it all ended. In 1147 the fanatic Islamic fundamentalists of Morocco, the Almohades, invaded Spain like a wave of locusts and destroyed the symbiosis between Muslims and Jews. The Golden Age, at least for the Jews of Spain, was suddenly and painfully over, and with it the perfect childhood of Moses Maimonides. He was only twelve years old.

The wall surrounding Córdoba. (Photo by Gregory Frux)

# 2

## Exiles in Their Own Land

> If I [God] am here everyone is here.
> If I am not here nobody is here.
>
> —*Hillel the Elder*

THE MAGHREB, comprising of the coastlands and the Atlas Mountains of Morocco, Algeria and Tunis, became one of the most violent regions of northwest Africa during the eleventh century. The Almoravids, a tribe of Saharan Berbers, employed religious reforms and military power to gain control of the area, establishing their capital in Marrakesh in 1062. They advanced over the Mediterranean, and eventually the entire Muslim Spain except Valencia fell under their rule. Surprisingly, when the wars ended, the relationship between Muslim Spain and the Maghreb became mutually beneficial, with strong cultural exchange.

Unfortunately, the peaceful situation did not last. It was changed by a well-educated and extremely religious man, Ibn Tumart. He was born in Morocco and traveled widely over the entire Muslim world, studying and acquiring new ideas. Eventually, Ibn Tumart developed a religious doctrine that was about to change Islam: a combination of the strict Unity of God and a scrupulous observance of Islamic law. His ascetic ideas appealed to the Berbers, and despite extensive persecution from the authorities, Ibn Tumart became the spiritual leader of a large number of followers.

In 1117, Ibn Tumart traveled as usual along the Maghreb. A

young man, Abd al Mumin, met him and absorbed his preaching. The new doctrine swept him away from his old world. He abandoned the idea of continuing his own studies and attached himself to the spiritual leader, together with many new followers. In 1120, a Berber confederation rose in the Atlas Mountains, based on the teaching of Ibn Tumart, and in 1121, Ibn Tumart proclaimed himself as the mahdi—meaning "the divinely guided one." When Ibn Tumart's second-in-command was killed in battle, Abd al Mumin took his place. In 1125 the Almohades began a military rebellion in the Atlas Mountains, and when Ibn Tumart died in 1130, Abd al Mumin became the leader of the Almohades, and took the title of caliph. The Almohades fought for twenty-two years, and finally won, conquering Marakesh in 1147. Until his death in 1163, Abd al Mumin worked on winning complete control of North Africa and Spain and enforcing the Almohades' violent ideas.

The Almohades spared no one. On their way from North Africa to Spain they left a bloody trail of dead and forcefully converted Christians and Jews. Muslims suffered as well at their hands. Even though the Almoravids were Berbers from North Africa just like the Almohades, the two groups did not share religious convictions. The Almohades despised the soft, luxury-loving Almoravids.

When they first invaded Spain, the Almohades' motto was: "No church and no synagogue." They gave non-Muslims only two alternatives: conversion or death. Later, they allowed a third option—emigration. Christians could go to Northern Spain and settle there with relative comfort, because it was under Christian rule. The Jews, however, expected persecution wherever they went. Many traveled to the Christian areas in Spain and to various cities in France, but the inhabitants did not welcome them. Other Jews elected to stay in areas still ruled by the Almoravids, but they knew it was only a matter of time until the Almohades would catch up with them. Once that happened, many were killed, and the others, faced with the grim alternative of submitting to Islam or leaving the city, feigned acceptance of Islam.

Fortunately, their duties as new Muslims required little

The Judería (Jewish Quarters) in Córdoba, Spain, birthplace of Maimonides.
(Photo by Gregory Frux)

*Right and below:* Outside view of the Great Mosque in Córdoba, seen against the wall surrounding the city.
(Photos by Gregory Frux)

effort. They had to accept monotheism, as represented by Allah; but since monotheism is the cornerstone of Judaism, the Jews did not consider the Muslims idolaters, and that eased the discomfort of the forced conversion. However, they also had to declare their belief in the Prophet Muhammad, and occasionally attend services at the mosques, two acts which were alien to Judaism. Still, this pretense only had to be observed in public. Unlike the later Spanish Christian Inquisitors, the Muslims did not check what the new converts did privately at home, so they were able to continue practicing Judaism with relative safety.

However, the Almohades destroyed the synagogues, with all their rich art and architecture. They also dismantled the Jewish schools in Córdoba, Lucena and Seville. Except for the forced converts, the Córdoban Jews dispersed, and many started a life of wandering, doing their best to blend with the Muslim society on the road and in the cities they temporarily stayed in. Fortunately, they easily disguised themselves as Muslims, because Jews normally wore the same clothes and turbans, and their Arabic was fluent. They knew that if they refused conversion, they had to face dismal poverty and perpetual danger on the road. Nevertheless, they turned their backs on their beloved city and left. One of the finest congregations in the history of Judaism came to an end.

RABBI MAIMON REFUSED to stay in Córdoba, preferring exile to pseudo conversion. He decided to avoid the Christian lands, where the language and culture were alien to him, and stay as long as possible in Muslim Spain. Leaving most of their possessions behind, the family set out with a group of refugees heading toward the port city of Almería. The exile caused a violent shock to Moses, who loved Córdoba deeply to the end of his days. He never lost this attachment, and mentioned it again and again in his letters, always giving the impression that he never stopped considering it his home. Emotionally, Moses remained an exile for his entire life.

If poverty, fear, hunger and exile were not enough, the realization of a horrifying calamity staggered Moses. Suddenly, he had no access to books. Rabbi Maimon's immense library, Moses' solace, his great love, the core of his being, was reduced to the few volumes they could carry with them on the road. It was at this time that Rabbi Maimon's tremendous emotional strength came to the aid of his desperate boy. He told Moses that his studies would never stop—no matter what. They would rest in various towns, he said, and find books at friends' homes. At other towns they would meet scholars and ask them to teach Moses on a temporary basis. The rest of the time, Rabbi Maimon promised, he would teach the boy orally, from memory.

The pact between these two extraordinary people worked. As they traveled by foot or donkey, rested in miserable inns and stayed occasionally at old acquaintances' homes, Rabbi Maimon continuously instructed Moses. The boy listened and absorbed his lessons. He trained his memory to retain vast amounts of information. In turn, he taught everything he could to his younger brother David, strengthening and reinforcing the learning experience. In later years, Moses commented that his memory, even in later life, was so perfect that he never needed notes. This probably is due thanks to the early hardship and mental adjustment to so much oral instruction. In the various cities they stayed in, Rabbi Maimon contacted teachers of secular subjects, and Moses managed to advance his studies of philosophy and the sciences with great success.

The period of wandering stretched into years. For a while, until 1151, they stayed in the port city of Almería. Not much is known about their circumstances there, except for one great friendship that was struck between Moses and Averroës, the Arabic philosopher from Córdoba. Averroës had to go into exile after his exegesis of the Qur'an was found to be too liberal. Like Moses, Averroës was the son of a judge. He was only nine years older than Moses, and the two young men had much in common, intellectually and spiritually. The friendship proved rewarding for both.

When the Almohades captured Almería the family was forced to flee again. They wandered for several years in a wasteland of devastated Jewish communities. They drifted from one city in Andalusia to another, settling in some places temporarily only to be told of the continuing horror of the invasion and the need to move on again. Somewhere on the road Rabbi Maimon's wife died, and he trudged on with his two sons and two young daughters, whose dates and places of birth are unknown. One was named Miriam, and scholars believe she married and stayed on in the Muslim West. There is a fragment of a letter from many years later from Miriam in the Cairo Geniza (a combination of storehouse, archive and a hiding place to preserve documents), where she complains to Moses about her son, who traveled far and did not write to her for a very long time, indicating that the connection between the brother and sister probably never ceased. The other sister's name is unknown, but we do know the identity of the man she later married in Egypt, the names of some of her sons, and a few facts about her later life. Little else is known about either of them, as it happens with all the women in Moses' life story.

The frustrating paucity of information about Moses' female relatives is due to a complicated set of circumstances. The customs at that time gave women as much privacy as possible. It was considered rude to discuss them, either in person or in writing, any more than was absolutely essential. Even in letters, one did not refer to a woman by name and never greeted her directly. In Moses' genealogical list, appearing in the Cairo Geniza, only the men are recorded. Women are not mentioned at all.

Moses also had an ambivalent relationship with women all his life. Not in the sexual respect; he was a heterosexual and had a conservative marriage. Emotionally, however, his writings present contradictions that are not easy to explain. On one hand, there is a serious controversy regarding wife beating. The controversy is based on one sentence in his writings, where he claims that if a wife willfully refuses to fulfil her domestic duties, she could be punished, even to the point of beating. This line caused a furor in many Jewish congregations even in his own days, particularly in France, because Jews in the West did not officially allow wife beating, though it was not an unusual "unofficial" practice. In another place he claims that even though a woman has the right to leave her house as she pleases, her husband would do well to encourage her not to do so more than twice a month, because a woman is most honored at home.

On the other hand, in specific judgments left in his responsa and in his books, Moses treated individual women with honor and respect well ahead of his time and culture. He repeated often that they were not slaves, that their husbands did not own them and that they had a right to property and divorce. He respected learning in women, and encouraged independence in poor women who had to support themselves. He also was one of the first letter writers to break the taboo of greeting a woman directly. He openly sent his regards and his blessings to the woman of the house in letters to friends and relatives.

How are Maimonides' contradictions to be understood? One must take any historic figure as a product of his time, i.e., Maimonides must be understood against the backdrop of twelfth-century social mores. In Muslim society of the period, physical punishment was the rule, not the exception. Adult males and females alike were regularly flogged as punishment for many minor offenses. It was as much a part of the social scene as parking tickets are today. Children were flogged in schools for any form of disobedience. Therefore, corporal punishment was not alien or objectionable as it is today. Jews lived in very much the same fashion. The Gaon of Baghdad, Samuel ben Ali, was known to have his many slaves regularly punish Jewish offenders by administering flogging. Also, in that society, most new wives were practically children. They came to their new homes as adolescent girls, and often, according to the literature, had a very difficult adjustment period, sometimes rebelling within the new home, sometimes actually running away back to their parents' home. Many were unwilling to do their part of the household chores and were not very cooperative with their mothers- and sisters-in-law. An adult male such as Moses would see corporal punishment as merely a way to educate a young person and help correct her wicked ways. He probably even saw it as kindness, based on the biblical advice to always correct a child's behavior and never spare the rod so as not to spoil the child.

These facts may not justify his contradictions to the modern reader, but in the end, even though his attitude was not always to our modern taste, Moses did much for the advancement of women's position in society and the improvement of their lot.

YEARS PASSED. He studied and he wrote, and even though much information is lost about the family's whereabouts during this time, we can keep track of Moses' growth and maturity through the writings he left us. During the years on the road, Moses wrote two original works. The first, at the age of sixteen, was an introduction to the terminology employed in logic and metaphysics, called the *Milloth Higgayon* (Treatise on Logical Terminology), based on the works of Aristotle. The second was a work about the rules of the calendar, called *Maamar ha-ibbur* (Essay on the Calendar). This work skillfully describes, in lucid, easy-to-understand language, the rationale, mechanics and astronomical principles of the Jewish calendar—an area in which *halachah* (Jewish law) and natural science are intermingled. This second book was written as a response to a request from an acquaintance. It launched a life-long tradition: Moses would write much of his later work as responses to questions from the religious community all over the Jewish world and he would write occasional essays dealing with current problems that faced the Jewish community, maintaining an extensive correspondence with scholars and community leaders. When he wrote the calendar book he was still in his early twenties. Jews, who venerated age and considered it a part of wisdom, did not usually recognize a youth as a religious authority. But they could not deny Moses' genius.

In addition, he researched the works of the *geonim* (singular, gaon), the scholars of the early Middle Ages, and collected the notes of his father and of Joseph ibn Migash, as preparation for a work of commentary on the Babylonian Talmud. Mostly he was interested in the practical law in the Talmud, the halachah, and in his early twenties had already finished writing notes on various tractates, including those of orders, festivals, laws of marriage, dietary laws and civil/criminal law. These early works reveal something of his character. One point of character was that he developed a habit of admitting to not knowing an answer to a problem. Moses never tried to extricate himself in a clever way from a difficult question. Instead, he often wrote, "I do not see how to explain this matter." It is interesting to note that Rashi, the great commentator from France, did the same. Both men obeyed the command of the rabbis of old: to teach their tongues to admit what they do not know. But the works of Rashi did not reach Spain at this time, and Moses could not have read them—it was entirely his own way. At twenty-two years old, already admired and honored, he could be so modest as to admit ignorance.

Those years also mark the time he started the *Commentary on the Mishna*, which would not be completed until 1168. To plan such an immense enterprise, to understand the need of the common man for a brief, clear, concise explanation of the Mishna without the complicated material of the Talmud, is another revealing point of his character. His deep and abiding need for precision and clarity in all things—and the scrupulous and searching exposition of Judaism in this and later works—would become a paradigm and challenge for future scholars and students of Jewish theology and philosophy. He named the work *Siraj*.[1] The name means "luminous light," which is an apt name for Moses' lifelong desire to shine a bright light on all that was shady and confusing.

Life on the road continued until they could no longer endure it. Their beloved homeland grew increasingly hostile and dangerous, and the refugees were exhausted. They were also spiritually disappointed. The Jews expected a miracle which did not happen; the Almohades were not struck dead by the Lord. Finally the family had to accept the painful reality: as Jews, they would never be able to settle anywhere in their beloved country and live free of fear. It was time to leave Spain—forever.

Miniature from Moses Maimonides' Mishneh Torah (Jewish religious code drafted in 1180). Southern European, ca. 1351.
(Giraudon/Art Resource, NY)

# 3

## Escape to the Maghreb

> He should leave everything he possesses and travel day and night
> until he finds a place where he can practice his religion,
> and the world is big and wide.
>
> —*Moses Maimonides*

WHY RABBI MAIMON chose to seek asylum in Fez is an interesting question. The Almohades occupied Fez, and persecuted the Jewish population, and many Jews sought escape from this city. Theoretically, the choice to live there made no sense, and scholars are still debating the question, eight hundred years after the fact. If, however, we examine the choice from a practical and psychological point of view, some answers emerge.

Fez represented a familiar territory to Rabbi Maimon. Jews had arrived in Morocco during the reign of King Solomon in 962–922 B.C.E., probably traveling in Phoenician ships. They lived under the Romans, Vandals, Byzantines and Arabs, never losing contact with other Jewish communities, and even gave financial support to the Jewish academies in Babylonia and Israel. Mutual respect existed between the Arabs and the Jews, just as in Spain. However, only fourteen years earlier, in 1145, with the Almohades' conquest of Fez, they gave the Jews their customary choice—convert, die or emigrate. Some Jews chose to die, others decided to leave. The largest number accepted Islam on pretense but continued to secretly practice Judaism.

The Muslim natives accepted the Almohades, though they detested the excessive puritanism the conquerors professed. They had little in common—the Almohades despised the inhabitants' comfortable lifestyle, love of beauty and enjoyment of luxuries and extravagance. Before the invasion the inhabitants of Fez had covered all the gold and silver decorations with plaster in one of the more sumptuous mosques, to save them from the invaders who would very likely have destroyed these works of art. The relationship between the two Muslim groups settled soon enough, albeit somewhat uncomfortably, but the inhabitants could do nothing for the persecuted Jews.

(The Jews of Fez firmly believed in an old legend about the mythical origin of the hatred between themselves and the Almohades, which revealed that the Almohades were the descendants of the Philistines. During the reign of King David, the Philistines escaped to North Africa from the wrath of Joab, his fierce commander-in-chief. In a small Moroccan village, an ancient monument called The Stone of Solomon bore an inscription of Joab's pursuing the Philistines to that specific point. According to this legend, the Almohades never forgot their hatred of the Jews, and enjoyed their revenge.)

Even under persecution, Rabbi Maimon preferred remaining in Muslim lands, and felt a strong aversion to the Christian lands. He had no acquaintances or business contacts in Christian lands, the culture and language were alien and no possible employment for himself or his sons existed. The Jews of Fez were old friends. The regular exchange of trade, scholarship and personal relations between Córdoba and Fez guaranteed that Rabbi Maimon could rely on a warm welcome and some means of employment. He even had some important contacts with influential people. For example, the famous Fez scholar, Rabbi Judah ibn Shoshan, was an old acquaintance who could do much for the Maimon family. Moses needed books, fellow scholars, Jewish activities to support him in his task of writing the *Commentary on the Mishna*. Rabbi Judah would supply all that. Moses also needed access to secular studies, and Fez, while losing its synagogues and churches, never lost its schools; the Almohades, though ardent religious fanatics, never objected to science and learning. Rabbi Maimon may also have had an influential contact in the court of the caliph, Abd al Mumin. The caliph's personal doctor, Ibn Tofail, was later succeeded by Averroës, their old friend from Almería. If the two physicians knew each other at that early date, which many scholars consider a distinct possibility, one letter of introduction from Averroës to Ibn Tofail would assure the family's acceptance and comfort among the Muslim population of Fez.

Another school of thought holds that all persecutions undergo cycles. During some periods they are intense and relentless; during other times they are lax and the minority regains a measure of freedom. These scholars speculate that the Maimon family went to Fez during a time of such laxity, when the Jews were less threatened. Fez also was probably more promising than Córdoba because in Fez the Maimons would be relatively strangers, and their disguise would be more likely to go undetected.

Some scholars speculate that Rabbi Maimon and his family actually converted to Islam. There is heated debate about this alleged conversion, based on a fact that emerged at a later date. When Moses moved to Egypt, a Moroccan Arab, Abul Arab ibn Moisha, informed the authorities that Moses was a Muslim while living in Morocco. This theory of conversion has few supporters, and Moses' most virulent opponents never brought this charge against him during his lifetime. It is safe to assume that the family never converted to Islam. They did disguise themselves as Muslims, and as they were strangers in Fez, the Muslim authorities did not suspect them for a long time. But such behavior was never considered unethical in Judaism. In many countries and in different eras, Jews were forced to disguise themselves to save their lives, and the rabbinical courts accepted such behavior as a safe solution to a chronic problem. The answer to Ibn Moisha's accusation is more likely that the Maimon family disguised themselves so well that he himself was duped into believing it.

THE MAIMON FAMILY needed to find a ship and prepare for the trip to Fez. Embarking on a sea voyage was no simple matter in those days, even on a seemingly short trip from Spain to Morocco, and despite the fact that medieval people traveled frequently. Most people preferred sea travel to land travel, but it took much thought and planning if one wanted to avoid danger and discomfort. The season naturally had to be taken into consideration. In the winter, the sea was closed to ships, and people used only land caravans. Ships usually set out in the spring and fall, so land caravans were also active in the summer.

Ships of various sizes traveled in convoys. The smaller ships sometimes traveled on their own, but more often accompanied a large ship. On arrival, the small ships took the passengers to shore. Often, they picked up survivors if the large ship sank. Many ships were indeed lost, but altogether not as many as might be expected. They were strong and suitable for the task.

Despite their strength, ships often could not complete a trip because of bad weather, and were forced to turn back. For merchants this represented a catastrophe—the loss of an entire business season. Furthermore, they could not recover the cost of customs and fares, and would lose all the money they had spent on provisions. Even when they set out to sea on time and managed to complete the trip, merchants often lost much of the merchandise. Even a mild storm might cause waves to wash over the decks and soak the merchandise. The saltwater permanently damaged fabrics, spices, salt, flour, wooden objects and many other perishable goods.

Pirates caused the greatest terror to sea travelers. When they took over a ship, many passengers had no chance of survival. Some were not killed: able-bodied men and women could be sold as slaves, and occasionally be bought back by their own countrymen. If a young woman passenger was beautiful, the pirates could make a good profit by selling her to a harem; she would rarely be heard from again. If the weather drove the ship to a hostile port, anything could happen to passengers, from simple confiscation of their goods to slavery or murder.

The Maimon family went on board a day before sail day, as was the custom. The decks hummed with activity: everyone pushing, talking, trying to find a place for themselves, arranging their goods and crying instructions to those who remained on shore.

Wicker baskets, rolled carpets and shapeless packages wrapped in cloth were stacked everywhere on deck, sailors ran back and forth, taking last minute care of the ship, passengers kept losing sight of their companions and nervously searched about. The amulet merchants swarmed the decks, taking advantage of the passengers' fear of the sea as they plied their thriving trade in magical items. The chaos lasted all day and well into the evening.

The night before departure had a special name—the Overnight Stay—and passengers spent it in writing letters, in prayers or in taking care of last-minute business. During the Overnight Stay Rabbi Maimon remembered and told his family the story he had heard about the famous poet, Judah Halevi's departure: Adverse winds held Halevi's ship in the port for four days before his trip to Egypt and Palestine. Bored and apprehensive, Halevi poured out his feelings and thoughts on paper, resulting in a lovely poem. When it was finished, he crumpled the paper impatiently and was about to throw it in anger into the sea, but fortunately, one of his many visitors requested it as a memento. Halevi, as always good-natured and obliging, handed it to him with a smile; the poem was preserved for posterity.

The Maimon family did not have as much luggage as some of the wealthier passengers, but they had brought all the equipment needed on the boat, such as bedding, household utensils and cutlery. Some large ships operating on the Indian Ocean had cabins, but most Mediterranean boats did not have such luxury. The passengers slept on their luggage, under the open sky. This did not present much of a hardship, though, because during sailing season the weather usually was fine with little if any rain.

The crew brought quantities of water on board just before departure, and stocked the ship with food. Passengers were occasionally permitted to purchase water and food, but they could not assume that it would last and neglect to bring their own. Experienced passengers generally brought dried bread and various dried fruits; they lasted for a long time and supplied good nutrition. Occasionally, if the food ran out on an extended trip, the captain had to cast anchor on a friendly shore and allow crew and passengers to purchase additional provisions. However, most captains disliked extending a trip by stopping, and only consented to do so in an emergency. The Maimon family packed some of the dried food inside wicker bags, tucked more among their linens and hoped it would last the trip. Most modern travelers would hardly be willing to exist for months on nothing but dried fruits and bread, but the medieval traveler was not choosy, and the Maimon family in particular was used to worse traveling conditions.

Once they set their luggage down and settled on board, Moses watched with disdain the thriving trade in magic, amulets and talismans. Until the last possible minute, well into the night, the amulet merchants stayed on board, selling magical trinkets and various magic formulas mysteriously scribbled on bits of paper. To see Jews resorting to magic bothered Moses; he simply could not understand their need for it. His faith in God was so deep, so abiding, that any deviation seemed to him unnecessary and somewhat ridiculous. Rabbi Maimon, with his usual kindness and tolerance, tried to remind Moses how frightened these people must be, and repeated to him the old saying about how "riding a ship," as the Arabs called sea travel, felt more like the experience of a worm riding on a splinter.

The family's most important possession was a little package containing letters of introduction. Travelers always carried such letters on journeys, and used them extensively for both business and social reasons. The letters would state the purpose of the bearer's journey; why the bearer needed help; what kind of assistance was required; why the receiver was the right person to provide help. A letters declared that the bearer was worthy of attention, and that the writer of the letter saw any such help as personal attention given to himself. Many examples of these polite letters, written almost to a formula, have been preserved. Medieval society thrived on social interaction, and these letters provided substantial help away from home. Few people dared venture a trip without another type of letter—the safe conduct letter (a letter from the authorities of the strange land that grants safe conduct)—used for safe passage through hostile territory. The Maimon family had to do without a safe conduct letter, and had done so for years, living by their wits on the road.

THE FAMILY'S TRIP WAS long, but mercifully uneventful, and even their food lasted. Moses passed the time by working on his book, and dreaming of a brighter future for the family. His thoughts returned often to the loss of Spain, but he steeled himself against despair and brooding, and forced himself into perfect faith.

Once in Morocco, they had to travel to Fez by land. Two things were certain. First, they could not travel alone. No one did, with robberies and murder so common on the road, so they had to join a caravan. Second, the caravan had to offer beasts for hire, because they could not walk such a distance, nor carry their heavy luggage. People did not like traveling on foot; only the very destitute walked. In general though, riding or walking were the only choices, because carriages were uncommon. Few people used horses. The higher ranks rode mules, the rest of the population rode donkeys. When traveling by water, many people even took their own saddle and headgear with them, and hired an animal at the beginning of the overland journey. Heavy luggage was carried by a beast of burden, such as a camel or an ox, and only a caravan could supply the Maimon family with that. On the road, whenever possible, people stayed in inns and caravansaries, which they could even book in advance. Needy travelers were accommodated in buildings provided by their religious community.

The Maimon family settled with a large caravan organized by Berbers. No one knew the Maimon family were Jews, as their Arabic was flawless and their clothes and turbans looked exactly like those worn by any Muslim passenger from Spain. They easily secured the donkeys, the camel and the food supplies, and as they were surrounded by so many people, felt reasonably safe. Their feeling was justified; the trip was uneventful, though long, tedious and exhausting. Finally, after what seemed like an eternity of heat, dust and discomfort, the tired family reached the city of their destination and gazed upon the walls of Fez. It was a place that would frighten any newcomer.

Locket with portrait of Moses Maimonides.
Copper, gilt, with silver relief. Italy about 1700.
(Art Rsesource, NY)

# 4

## Behind the Walls of Fez

Let us further grasp every occasion to perform good and pious deeds.
For the time to work is now, while we live on earth;
the time for our reward will come later, when we are in heaven.

—*Rabbi Maimon ben Joseph*

THE MAIMON FAMILY entered a dark, foreboding city. It took a few minutes for their eyes to adjust to the gloom after the bright North African sun that had followed them mercilessly during the trip. Moses' heart sank as he looked at the miserable narrow streets, strewn with filth, and the houses that possessed high walls, hiding the life behind them with dreary secrecy. The memory of the charming, flower-filled cities of Andalusia burst upon him with unexpected power.

Suddenly Moses smiled. It dawned on him that living in Fez offered certain advantages for refugees. Hiding, or leading any kind of a secret life, was relatively easy in this desolate place. The narrow, winding streets permitted easy escape at necessary moments. The houses' high façades would never tell tales about the forbidden studies and dangerous religious practices taking place inside. People skulked in the dusty streets, wearing thick veils; even the men chose to wear them, because the Berbers considered a bare face in public as most unseemly. One could never be sure if a passerby was a Jew or a Muslim. In such a bleak place, Jews could easily mingle and hide their identity, particularly if they were strangers and no one knew anything about them. They could almost disappear.

No matter how unpleasant and uninviting the city looked, Moses thought, friends lived here. Friends who would show the family how to survive and obtain work. His father would find scope for his scholarship and interest in community affairs, perhaps use his expertise as a dayyan. His brother David, who already showed a shrewd understanding of commerce, could apprentice to a merchant and learn the precious stone and pearl business, which interested him. Miriam and her sister would finally live in a proper home, receive training in the domestic subjects they needed but had not been able to learn on the road and could expect better prospects for marriage and a settled future. Moses envisioned himself studying and writing in peace, visiting libraries and schools, talking to fine scholars and reading new and exciting books.

The family settled in the part of Fez which is now known as the "Old City," in a strong house with massive walls. Between the floors, a horizontal row of thirteen stones protruded just under the windows. A mystery surrounds these stones. Moses and Rabbi Maimon placed a copper bowl on each stone, the purpose for which is disputed. Some scholars think that they used these bowls for astronomical research and calculations of the calendar, and this theory fits. The Talmud regards the study of astronomy as almost a divine command, and Rabbi Maimon was known to have been interested in astronomy. With Moses the subject constituted a true passion. Various legends and oral tales regarding the thirteen bowls also exist.

One particularly charming account is taken from a story cycle written in Hebrew. According to the legend Moses was the wisest man of his generation. Wishing to know the time, but, as clocks did not exist, he placed twelve copper bowls outside his window, and arranged one more bowl above them. Each hour, the thirteenth bowl hit the appropriate number of bowls. When it was one o'clock, the bowl hit only one other bowl. When it was two o'clock, the bowl hit two other bowls, etc. The thirteenth bowl magically knew the hour, and thus it was Moses always knew the time. Years after Moses left Fez, the bowls continued to tell time, and the Jews of Fez considered them holy. When Moses died, the bowls are said to have never rang again.

The family's hopes about their new home were justified, and settling in Fez was not too difficult. Moses continued working on his *Commentary on the Mishna*, and Rabbi Judah ibn Shoshan was indeed instrumental in aiding him, supplying books and introducing him to various scholars. They became close friends. Marvelous opportunities for secular studies presented themselves as well. Many distinguished scholars, famous for their knowledge in mathematics, philosophy and the sciences welcomed him. Fez also had many eminent Arab physicians, and Moses pursued medical studies, a subject that had interested him since childhood.

IT WAS NOT LONG however, before the family realized the Jewish community of the Old City was in disarray. Observing Judaism openly was a cause for execution, and many Jews pretending to be Muslims, continued practicing Judaism in secret. But the years of persecution caused not only physical and economic, but psychological hardship as well. The Jews began to doubt their own religion, and worry that perhaps Islam represented the true religion after all, with Muhammad replacing the biblical Moses as the true prophet.

To make matters worse at such a difficult time, a most unfortunate incident staggered the Jewish community. A famous rabbi, well known for his piety and scholarship, wrote an epistle denouncing any Jew who publicly professed to be a Muslim but practiced Judaism in secret. The epistle was prompted by a Jew from the Mahgreb, possibly even a resident of Fez, who had requested the rabbi's opinion on the conduct of the Jews who saved their lives by repeating the verbal formula requested by the Almohade authorities. The formula consisted of stating, "There is no God but Allah, and Muhammad is His prophet." The rabbi promptly sent his answer.

The epistle thundered and pontificated with an unbelievable degree of intolerance. The rabbi claimed that God did not even listen to the prayers of such sinners, and their praying was not only

futile, but a crime against religion. A man who repeated the formula was no longer a real Jew, but a heathen, even if he fulfilled all
the Torah's obligations. The rabbi encouraged the suffering
Maghreb Jews to sacrifice their lives to Judaism and die as martyrs.

No one noticed that the rabbi himself stayed in his own safe
area, never suggesting to join and lead the martyrs. Somehow,
his credibility was never challenged, and the epistle, which was
read by everyone, caused confusing agony among the Jews.
Some ceased to pray, denying themselves this strong psychological relief. Many considered complete conversion, thus threatening to destroy the Jewish community in Morocco in its entirety.

Neither Rabbi Maimon nor Moses felt they could tolerate
this abuse, and both wrote epistles as a response. Rabbi Maimon's famous Letter of Consolation, written in 1160, was a love
letter from a great man to his people. Israel, he wrote, is still the
beloved child of God. God is not a fickle being who loves only
for a while. His promise to His people will live through the centuries, and He will never cease to listen to their prayers. Even if
they could not pray during the set times in the synagogues, he
wrote, it did not matter. A silent prayer from the heart will
always be welcomed by a merciful God.

> And it is necessary that we should rely upon God, and believe
> in Him, and no doubt His promises, just as we do not doubt
> His existence, nor should we fear that He will cast us off
> when he has promised to draw us near unto Him, nor should
> the great prosperity of the nations terrify us, or what they
> assert, or what they hope for, because we confide in God, and
> put faith in His Promises. And in spite of their victory over
> us, and their anger against us, and our subjegation to them,
> and the renewal of our calamities with the renewal of day and
> night . . . we must still reflect upon that which He has prom-
> ised us, and upon that which we, and then the weary souls
> will have rest, and their fears allayed, for there must needs be
> repose and healing after this unhappiness, there must needs
> be enlargement after this staritness. . . .[1]

The letter contained beautiful imagery and metaphors; one of them described God's law as a cord that stretched from heaven to earth, so that those who drown in the sea of captivity could grasp it and be saved. Of course the best practice was to grasp it with your whole hand, but if you were forced to barely cling to it with your fingertips, surely you had more hope than a person who would let go of the rope completely?

This Letter of Consolation by Moses' father, a wonderful example of heartfelt tolerance, was based wholly on the feeling and relationship between God and man and on pure faith. In 1162, Moses would write another kind of letter. It is best known as the Epistle on Apostasy (also known as Epistle on Conversion).[2] He composed a rational letter based on the Law, and illustrated it with his own special type of logic. Moses claimed that the accusation and clinical denouncement by the famous rabbi, who greatly increased the anguish and despondency of the Jews under Almohade rule, was a misinterpretation of Judaism. Using Talmudic passages, he proved that it was not a sin to disguise oneself in times of religious persecution to save one's life. He brought forward precedence from Roman times, with such examples as great Jewish leaders who had had to take this difficult road. No Jew in his right mind could possibly claim that these great people ceased to be Jews. In addition, Moses cited the Talmud and the Bible in the defense of silent prayer, and mentioned instances where forced apostasy was accepted and even rewarded by God. He used rigorous halachic reasoning and interpretation, as well as legal, theological and rhetorical arguments to discredit his opponent's views.

The type of apostasy required by the Muslims, Moses wrote, did not require transgression of God's laws. Only lip service was required. Moses could see why a person would martyr himself if a serious offence was required. But the Talmud declared only three capital offences that would justify martyrdom: idolatry, unchastity and murder. One had to be reasonable when only a verbal formula was required.

Naturally, he wrote, it was preferable to worship God in

peace, and if possible, a person should leave the country of persecution and move to a place where he could live safely as a Jew. Using the excuse of waiting for the Messiah for staying in a hostile land was wrong, he wrote. But if a person could not leave the country of persecution, all he needed to do was to make sure he never profaned the name of God, and to pursue Judaism secretly.

Finally, using his medical knowledge, Moses dispassionately claimed that the writer of the epistle could not possibly be a man of sound mind and body. The rabbi must be sick, either in body or in mind. There was no need to listen to him.

The Epistle on Apostasy saved the Jewish community in Morocco from further demoralization and disintegration. By following Moses' advice, the Jews overcame their despair, and instead of converting to Islam or choosing to martyr themselves by dying, they lived the double life that allowed them to survive until better conditions prevailed. When writing this remarkable epistle, Moses was in his mid-twenties. Allowing himself to strongly criticize a rabbi, a man of high position and older than himself, was unusual within the Jewish community. To coolly state that this rabbi was insane or ill, was even more surprising. Respect for one's elders was strongly ingrained. This is one of the occasions when Moses' inner core of pride, perhaps a touch of arrogance even, shows through his genuine efforts to be humble. Some scholars deny such an accusation of arrogance, saying that he only wrote this epistle out of love for his suffering people, that he could not resist doing so, but this makes no sense. Any ordinary young Jewish man of that time would have considered his father's Letter of Consolation perfectly sufficient. Perhaps he would have asked to contribute something to the letter, but no more. But Moses was not an ordinary young man. He lived by a different code, and his relationship with Rabbi Maimon, who seemed to understand him better than anyone else, was more than the ordinary father and son relationship.

The epistle shows that Moses was already considering moving away from Fez, though not immediately. He continued with his work on the *Commentary on the Mishna*, with the encouragement of Rabbi Judah ibn Shoshan, and made progress with his rabbinical studies. He also advanced with his philosophical, scientific and medical studies, assisted by his Muslim friends. At home, the family observed Jewish law meticulously, and outside of the house they disguised themselves successfully as Muslims. They went to the mosque when needed, such as during the time of Ramadan or other specially holy Muslim days, but did not offer prayers. Moses did not consider the Muslims idolatrous, as they believed in the Unity of God, and the disguise did not lie heavily on his conscience. This double life might have gone on indefinitely, when suddenly disaster struck.

In 1163, Abd al Mumin passed away. His successor, Abu Yakub Yussuf, accelerated the persecution of the Jews. The violence escalated for the next couple of years, and Rabbi Judah ibn Shoshan, a pseudo convert like most everyone else, was suddenly seized by the authorities and accused of relapsing into Judaism. No appeal was permitted for relapsing, and Rabbi Judah was horribly tortured and then executed. As a close friend of the great rabbi, Moses was also arrested and accused of the same crimes. He would have undoubtedly been executed if it were not for his friend, the scholar Abul Arab ibn Moisha. The brave man intervened and demanded of the authorities to free Moses. Miraculously, the authorities agreed, but the family could not stay in Fez—it was just a matter of time before any of them would be arrested again. Next time there might not be a lucky deliverance; one more time, they had to prepare for escape.

*Above:* Bab al-Nasr (Gate of Victory) in Cairo. Like the Bab al-Fatuh (Gate of Conquests) below, this gate was built in the fortifications by the Fatimids.
(Photo by Mary Knight)

*Right:* Bab al-Futuh (Gate of Conquests) also in Cairo.
(Photo by Mary Knight)

# 5

## Eretz Israel

My heart is in the East and I am at the ends of the West. How can I taste what I eat, how can I enjoy it? How can I fulfill my vows and pledges while Zion is in the bindings of Edom and I am in the bonds of Arabia? Easier it seems to me to abandon all the good things of Spain, as more precious would it be to behold the dust of the ruined Temple.

—*Judah Halevi*

AN OLD LEGEND tells a most heroic story about Moses' escape from Fez. According to the tale, Moses was functioning as a dayyan and worked next door to a Muslim judge who hated the Jews. The judge once claimed that if a Jew touched the clothes of a Muslim, the Muslim must bathe to purify himself and change his clothes. Moses refused to see the Jews humiliated, and waited for his chance to return the insult.

One day, a Jew came to consult Moses. The Jew owned two vats, one of oil, the other of wine. The previous day, a mouse had fallen into the oil and drowned, and a Muslim passed by and touched the vat of wine. Could the Jew still use the oil and the wine? Moses, as usual surrounded by many listeners, deliberated the two problems. Finally, he said that the Jew may remove the mouse and use the oil. As for the wine, he continued, this was another matter. A Jew was forbidden to drink wine that had been touched by a Muslim. The Jew had to discard the vat of wine.

As Moses intended, the judge next door heard his decision. Furiously, the judge rose and screamed at the crowd that Moses considered a dead mouse a purer entity than a living Muslim! Such a man must be destroyed! The enraged and violent crowd began chasing Moses through the streets. He ran to the first city gate, whereupon God sent a pride of lions to his rescue, which tore many of his pursuers to pieces. The lions' attack slowed the crowd and Moses managed to run to the second city gate. At the second gate, God sent him swords, which brandished themselves in the air and stabbed some of the pursuers. During the miraculous fight, Moses ran to the third city gate. There, fire blazed through the gate and burned many of the pursuers. Finally Moses made his way to the fourth and last city gate, and saw that a huge boulder blocked it! Trusting in God, Moses hurled himself into the stone, and God made him magically disappear through it—and reappear in Egypt—safe and sound.

Unfortunately, this is not how it happened; Moses did not brave a crowd, all alone. Instead, he had to consider his aging father, who could not run very fast, and his young sisters who would be much hampered by their voluminous clothes if they had to run. (A respectable girl in the Maghreb wore many layers of clothing, and would not consent to wear men's clothes if her life depended on it.[1]) So instead of enjoying a number of quick and convenient miracles, the family had to rely on its extensive experience as travelers and fugitives.

Hiding under the darkness of the night, the family crept through the ominous, deserted streets. They did not carry lanterns, and whenever they heard a sound, hid themselves in the deep shadows. Finally they stole out of Fez.

They walked all night, putting as much distance between themselves and Fez as they could. To maintain secrecy, they could not join a caravan or even prepare donkeys for the trip. Fortunately, the Almohades kept the roads in good repair, and even without donkeys they could reach their destination. Except for food, they took little; anything large and heavy had to be left behind. Moses' brother David carried some gemstones with him—all their money was invested into this portable commodity. They saved a couple of books, some clothes and what would matter most to future generations—an unfinished manuscript tucked safely into Moses' robe.

They hid themselves during the days and marched through

the nights, until they reached the outskirts of Ceuta. A bustling port town on the northern edge of Morocco, Ceuta served as a center of commerce and scholarship and home to a Jewish congregation. The family planned to hide there for a while, and prepare for boarding a ship: they had decided to go to Palestine, which was under Christian rule at the time. Much as they still disliked the idea of living in Christian lands, under the circumstances, it was decided, it would be a good idea to be as far removed from the Almohade authorities as possible.

Despite the fear and loss, Moses noticed that a queer sort of happiness sustained him throughout the ordeal. He knew the feeling fed on nothing but wishful thinking, because Palestine did not welcome Jews at the time, but he could not resist it. No matter who held the land, it was still *Eretz Israel*,[2] where it all began. It represented the core of Judaism to Moses, where God had made the Covenant with His people, and the land of David the King, his ancestor. Moses would finally see it, would walk its sacred soil. More than anything else in the world, he wanted to settle there and never leave. But even if he could not stay, he would carry that treasured experience in his heart for the rest of his life.

The family entered Ceuta at night, and found an inn to hide in until they could book passage on a boat and prepare some provisions. It did not take long, because fortunately the time of year was right—spring time. On a dark Saturday night, the family stealthily boarded a ship heading toward Palestine. The year was 1165, and Moses had reached his thirtieth year a few days before.

The sea voyage from Ceuta to the port city of Acre generally lasted about a month; the family expected to celebrate the Feast of the Weeks in Palestine. The captain planned to hug the coast, which would provide a reasonably safe trip. Or so they hoped. Particularly since the vessel was the same type of large, secure ship they sailed in when they traveled from Almería to Morocco. For six days all indeed went well. The family, relieved from their fear of persecution, relaxed and enjoyed the voyage; Moses worked steadily on his project. One morning, peacefully writing, he raised his eyes to see an ominous dark cloud forming in the distance. With frightful suddenness, a terrible storm gathered and pounced on the helpless ship. The furor of the sea forced the panicking sailors to jettison the cargo overboard, a common practice during heavy storms in those days.

As a mere passenger, Moses could do nothing to help the situation; the experienced sailors fought the sea. He knew this could be his last hour, and terror struggled with faith in his heart. But this was not the first time he was in mortal danger. He slipped away to a deserted area, calmed his mind and prayed to God to save the boat and everyone on it. A letter he wrote later shows his interesting, unusual approach to communication with God:

> On Sunday night, the fourth of the month of Iar, I went to sea, and on Saturday, the tenth of the month of Iar of four thousand, nine hundred and twenty five years of the creation, 1165, a giant wave came to drown us. A storm of great fury raged over the sea, and I vowed: those two days[3] I will keep a complete fast, myself and my household and all that will be with me, and I will command my sons do so till the end of their generations, and also to give charity as much as they can. I vow: I will be alone each tenth of Iar, I will see no human being but pray and read all day by myself. And as I have found no one during that day at sea but the Lord, so I will not see any human being and sit with him unless I am forced to do so.
>
> And on Sunday night, the third of the month of Sivan, I left the sea in peace and came to Acre, escaping persecution, and reached Eretz Israel. And this day, I vowed, will be a day of jubilation, festivity, and gifts to the poor, from myself and my house till the end of the generations.

Vowing to keep the day as a fast day for oneself and the generations to come, including the command for charity and giving thanks, was a normal reaction to danger. Many Jews would adopt this behavior under such circumstances, and probably did so on this very boat. But the other statement is curious, and it reveals his relationship to his God. Moses made a personal vow to keep away from any human company, and spend the tenth of Iar every year alone with God, praying and studying, just as he was all alone with Him during the storm. This personal relationship with God permeated Moses' being, from early childhood to the last day of his life.

The storm subsided as suddenly as it started, and no one on the ship was seriously harmed. As Moses continues to tell in his letter, expressing the drama of the events so well, the family eventually reached the port of Acre, safe and sound, on the third of Sivan on the Jewish calendar. Moses vowed to keep this date as a day of celebration, rejoicing and distribution of charity by himself, his household and all the generations of his children.

HUNDRED OF SHIPS from all over the known world filled the port of Acre. They brought slaves and weapons and took back spices, silk clothes and Eastern luxuries of every kind. Christian pilgrims came continuously to worship in the holy land; many churches played their bells, distressing the Jewish travelers who often cried and tore their clothes at the sound of the bells and sight of the spires. The Maimon family gingerly stepped into the little boat that would take them over the blue water into the city, and tried to ascertain that the luggage that was lowered into it with ropes was really their own. Leaving the ship felt even more chaotic than embarking it, but at least this would be the last stage of the journey.

Acre under the Crusaders struck Moses as a beautiful, cosmopolitan city. The middle class dwelt in pleasant stone houses, fitted with glass windows and roof gardens, and with plumbing that was almost as efficient as that of Spain. Merchants and craftsmen from many countries lived and worked in separate streets, designated for their various specialities. The nobility occupied palaces and castles, surrounded by moats and walls. The city teemed with life, full of pilgrims, peddlers, merchants and knights going about their business, and was surrounded by a wall, so wide that two chariots could ride side by side on top of it. The Mediterranean rhythmically beat the city wall with its gleaming blue waves that sparkled under the glorious sunshine of the region, brighter than the glow of Spain, softer than the harsh glare of the Maghreb.

The Jewish community in Acre numbered only two hundred families, yet it proved to be the largest in Palestine. Only about a thousand families existed in all of Palestine. In Jerusalem no congregation existed at all—Jews were not permitted to settle there under Amalric, the king of Jerusalem. The family stayed with Rabbi Jaffet ben Eliyahu the dayyan, the well-respected head of the community. He was something of a celebrity, as mentioned by Rabbi Benjamin of Tudela in his famous book, *The Itinerary of Benjamin of Tudela*. Rabbi Jaffet ben Eliyahu and Moses became close friends, and later in life continued corresponding. Rabbi Jaffet even traveled with the family to visit Jerusalem.

In Acre, Moses devoted the usual time to his studies. He observed the rites practiced by the Palestinian Jews, which were somewhat different from those of Spain and Morocco, and found ancient talmudic texts he had never encountered before. He actually made a change in his *tephillin* (or phylacteries—the two small leather boxes attached to the body during prayer) following the opinions of various geonim, or scholars, in Jerusalem. As usual, he alternated his Judaic studies with secular subjects, and explored the local flora and the architecture of Palestine.

Despite his longing for, or perhaps because of his high expectations, Palestine disappointed Moses. The country was overrun by Christian immigrants (often fugitives from the law in other lands), opportunistic fortune hunters and soldiers for hire. Naturally, he did not associate with such people. However, he made the mistake of keeping away from the decent Christians as well. Theoretically, he knew that the Christians followed the Bible, but the statues and paintings of Mary, Christ and the saints struck him as idols, and therefore he could not rid himself of the feeling that the Christians were heathens. This attitude was different from his tolerance toward Muslims, whom he did not see as idolaters because of what he perceived as a stronger monotheistic approach. Consequently, Moses never really knew the Christians very well. He began to question his reasons for staying in Palestine or leaving it.

Either way, he wished to see as much of Palestine as he could. More than anything else he wanted to visit Jerusalem, see the site of the Temple, pray at the Western (or Wailing) Wall. Rabbi Maimon, Rabbi Jaffet and his brother David went with Moses, despite the serious dangers experienced on the roads in Palestine. He spent three days in Jerusalem, praying, studying the architecture of the ancient city, looking at all the places he read about in the Bible. Then, he visited Hebron, where the graves of the Patriarchs were located in a cave, and spent a few days contemplating the site.

At this point the family already knew they could not stay in Palestine, and began to form the idea of moving to Egypt. Within such a small and weak Jewish community Moses could not find sufficient resources for his studies, or scholars to associate with. Nor could the family think of a way to make a living there. Two scholars and a fledgling gem merchant had little to offer in Palestine. And at thirty years of age, Moses was still a bachelor. Few suitable marriage candidates existed in Palestine for himself and his siblings, and they felt they could not wait any longer.

Some early writers speculated that Moses was married before he came to Palestine, and that his wife died there, and a few modern scholars agree with this possibility, but this is extremely unlikely. The early writers may have wanted to create a first wife because the Jewish community considered it unseemly for a young man not to be married, and they did not want to find any flaws of character in a revered leader. But Moses was just a human being who underwent many trials in his thirty years, and under the burdens of exile, wandering and poverty, could probably not find the time and money to marry. Remaining a bachelor, however, was not acceptable to him or his religious beliefs, and the pressure to marry would constitute a very strong reason for him to move to a large, community where he could find the means to do so.

The painful decision to move on hurt almost as much as

leaving Córdoba, and proved particularly hard to accept after so many disappointments and suffering. Moses dearly wanted to settle in Palestine, not only because the sacredness of the land meant so much to him, but because, in line with his messianic/nationalistic thinking, he considered a permanent and continuous presence of a Jewish habitat in Palestine as a sign that God would not abandon his Chosen People, and he wanted to be a part of this presence. It mattered so much to him that later he requested to be buried in Tiberias, a town by the lake Kineret, where other Jewish scholars were buried.

While the never-ending chain of disappointments and hardships began to wear Moses down, it certainly did not break his spirit. He was determined that nothing would prevent him from his studies, his writing and his yet unexpressed, but deeply felt mission to educate and enlighten his fellow men to the best of his ability. The thought sustained him in moments of depression, a condition he was to suffer with throughout his life.

The rest of the family accepted the move to Egypt much more readily. Rabbi Maimon fully understood how Moses felt about Palestine, and would have been happy to stay there if it were possible. However, Rabbi Maimon began to weaken with age and perpetual health problems. The thought of the good doctors, an easier lifestyle and decent income opportunities, all of which awaited the family in Egypt, helped to cheer him up despite the disappointment of leaving Palestine.

David welcomed the move. Excellent opportunities existed in Egypt for a young, intelligent and enterprising merchant, both professionally and socially. He started forming solid plans for their life in Egypt, which he later implemented successfully. One sister, Miriam, got married somewhere along the road and did not come to Egypt with them, but there is no certainty about where her wedding took place. (This is the sister from whom Moses received a letter written many years later from somewhere in the Muslim West, which survives in the Geniza documents, complaining that her son has traveled and did not write to her for a long time.)

There is not a single document telling how the second sister felt about moving to Egypt. But is can be safely assumed that the young girl looked forward to a large, busy community that offered the cheerful society of many new girlfriends, excellent shopping and many eligible young men who would be quite interested in the daughter of the celebrated Rabbi Maimon. Such a life of possibilities would have been more appealing than the grim reality in Palestine, without even her sister to keep her company.

Land caravans left regularly from Jerusalem, but like most travelers of the time the family preferred sea voyages. True, they were apprehensive about it after the horrible storm they experienced on their way to Palestine, but in Acre they could secure passage on an "Alexandian." These were large, comfortable vessels, called so because they plied between Alexandria and the rest of the Mediterranean. The Alexandrian ships were considered the safest, and much superior to the smaller coastal ships.

Returning to Acre with Rabbi Jaffet, they arranged for the trip. Their new friend, though sorrowful to see the family leave, sympathized with their motives and wished them well. They would maintain the friendship for life, and correspond regularly.

The family boarded the ship, and after a short and uneventful voyage they perceived the silhouette of the great lighthouse through the mists. The Alexandrian glided majestically into the impressive port it shared its name with.

Front view.

Entrance.

The thousand year-old Ben Azra Synagogue, where the Cairo Geniza was found.
(Photos by Mary Knight)

Back view.

# 6

## Interlude in Alexandria

> She is the most beautiful city in the world; there hath been none like her,
> even the stars of God go envious of her beauty.
>
> —*Lord Dunsany*

RABBI BENJAMIN of Tudela described Alexandria as an international, cosmopolitan city, and a center of commerce and study. It contained many beautiful palaces, elegant public buildings and private homes, and had many unusual features. He called it "a trading city of all nations," and told of each nation having its own storehouse. The layout and architecture impressed him, and he admired its builder, Alexander the Great, for his deep understanding of such matters. The streets were so unusually wide and straight, that a person standing at one gate at the beginning of a street, could see the gate ending it well over a mile away. The long pier, which Rabbi Benjamin described as a "king's highway," stretched into the sea, ending with a large and efficient lighthouse. Another accomplishment impressed Rabbi Benjamin even more—the city boasted more than twenty academies, each serving many students. The most famous was the Academy of Aristotle, built just outside the city.

The surviving literature shows the Alexandrians as a most attractive people: charming, luxury loving and easy going. Neither Muslims nor Jews adhered to the religious and moral commands as strictly as the citizens of the Maghreb and visitors often succumbed to their pleasant way of life. Judah Halevi, the grand old man of Jewish poetry, spent some time in Alexandria on his way from Spain to Palestine. He was not a young man at the time, and had left Spain to move to Israel because he wished to become more Godly. Before leaving Spain, he had vowed most solemnly to never again write a frivolous poem, never a love song or a wine song, but to devote all his creative energy to religious poetry. His intentions were undoubtedly holy, but when he encountered the Alexandrian women, his beauty-loving poet's eye certainly roved a little, and he left us a very secular poem showing his feelings toward the lovely girls. It describes their gazelle-like grace, their white arms, too delicate to support the heavy jewelry they wore, the power that their gazes exerted on the beholder, and so on. Half ashamed, he apologized for his unseemly writing. It is a marvelous poem, sensuous and warmhearted, and it makes any reader smile at the humanity of the great poet, swayed from his honorable intentions by a joyful experience.

Moses did not share such appreciation. He retreated from the sensual into his own philosophical universe, and did not approve of the lax lifestyle of the Alexandrians. It is easy to idolize such behavior by crediting it entirely to Moses' high morality. But his severe judgement may have also been psychologically related to the many years of deprivation and want that repressed the spirit of the young man. Such an early life could not be easily discarded by a sensitive, impressionable individual like Moses. The sudden change in circumstances might have caused two different approaches. He could have happily surrendered to the new easy lifestyle, or adopted a strong puritanical disdain, combined with a sense of sin and guilt. Moses reacted in the latter style, and withdrew from his surroundings. As a young man, he could not freely associate with young women anyway; actual contact (at least in theory) was prohibited. But he could have socialized a little more, enjoyed the sight of these beautiful people, and above all, he certainly could have arranged for a speedy marriage. He did none of these.

His brother David reacted quite differently to their new life. He quickly mingled with the community, met many people and married very soon after their arrival. As usual, we do not know his bride's name. But from a letter Moses later received from David it is clear that this was a happy and loving marriage. David was never one to adhere to society's rules too carefully, and in the letter he defied all decorum and tradition by sending a loving message to his wife and children.

The two brothers continued to live in the same household with their father and sister even after David's marriage. Extended families often lived together, though nuclear families existed as well in Egypt. It makes sense that the Maimon family did not wish to separate after all their years together on the road. Following his brother's marriage, Moses acquired new female relatives with whom he was permitted to associate freely, not only David's wife, but her mother and sisters as well. These women would have been delighted to help the young, handsome and well-connected scholar find a suitable bride among their wide circle of suitable girls.

Moses' continued unmarried state is a puzzling matter. Marriage was one of the chief reasons for his coming to Egypt, and yet, there is no evidence of a wife. Of course the legends try to remedy the situation. One legend claims he did marry, had two children, and lost his entire family under tragic circumstances, bearing the sorrow nobly. However, both the family and tragedy seem to be only another myth. Moses himself never mentioned this lost family—nor do any of his contemporaries—in letters to him or about him. His Fustat family, on the other hand, was mentioned often. In a letter written much later, Moses did mention the death of a little girl with great sorrow. However, the little girl undoubtedly was the first child he had with the woman he later married in Fustat, born some years before his son Abraham. If Abraham's mother did not give birth to this little girl, it would seem that Moses was married for full ten years before Abraham was born as his first child. It is possible, of course, but not very likely.

Whatever the circumstances, Moses did not find a wife in Alexandria. However, if he meant to retreat entirely into his studies, it was not to be; he was slowly drawn into the public eye by his scholarship, writings and interest in community affairs.

THE POLITICAL SITUATION in Egypt was complicated, with the last Fatimid caliph, El Adid, sitting on the throne, blissfully unaware of the impending upheaval that would soon start. The Fatimids were Shiites; the majority of their subjects were Sunnites. This combination would always trigger trouble, anyway, but it also further complicated the relationship between Muslims and Jews. The Karaites, considered a heretical Jewish sect, were the cause of additional problems, and with their tremendous wealth and power, strongly influenced the regular Jewish community. The Karaites enjoyed a favored position with the Fatimids. Shiites accepted only the written Qur'an, and rejected all Muslim oral tradition and Karaites accepted only the written Bible, and rejected all Jewish oral tradition. This similar religious view created a bond between the Shiites and the Karaites. They saw eye-to-eye on many subjects, religious as well as secular. Nevertheless, as the Karaites had no official leader, they were put under the head of the Jewish community, the *nagid* (roughly translated as "prince," though it can also mean a judge). Friction and trouble never ceased between the two Jewish communities.

The Jewish community in Egypt enjoyed complete autonomy under the leadership of the nagid. He appointed judges, rabbis and cantors, represented Jews to the government and generally assumed responsibility for the entire community. He sat up the courts in the cities and small towns, issued religious rulings, regulations and excommunications, and directed the talmudic academy. Almost every nagid enhanced his reputation by serving as the court physician.

The position of a nagid existed for a few hundred years before Moses came to Egypt, but when he arrived there was no one occupying the office, due to a particularly troublesome situation that occurred some years before. At that time, the nagid, Samuel ha-Nagid, a just, well-educated man, occupied the seat. His community greatly admired him, and Judah Halevi wrote songs in his honor, describing him in glowing terms. But the

Fatimid rule at the time proved corrupt enough to be suscepti-
ble to bribes, and in 1159, an ambitious and unscrupulous Jew
called Yahua Zuta, who wanted the office for himself, denounced
Samuel ha-Nagid to the caliph, claiming that Samuel was a traitor. The statement was accompanied by a neat sum of one thousand drachmas. The caliph removed Samuel from office and
gave the position to Zuta. Worse, he threw Samuel in jail for
sixty-six days, thus hastening the old man's death.

Zuta's reign did not last long, but it caused a lot of hardship.
He squeezed money and property out of the outraged community by various illegal means, and his judgments were corrupt or
at least inappropriate. The complaints finally forced the caliph
to reconsider his position and reinstate Samuel, but after his jail
sentence Samuel became very ill, and died in 1160. Zuta immediately set out to regain his power. He told the caliph that
Samuel had left behind a hidden treasure, and that if the caliph
reinstated Zuta, he would deliver the money to the caliph's
hands. The scheme did not work, because no such treasure ever
existed, and the caliph, finally disgusted with Zuta and his
schemes, commanded him to leave the office, and never to show
his face in court. After that, the nagid's office was to remain
empty until Moses finally took its seat.

For a little while, Moses stuck to his decision to disassociate
himself from political affiliations and concentrate on his studies
and writing. However, as had been the case in Palestine, he
quickly noticed the lack of Jewish scholarship in Alexandria. The
secular academies allowed him the studies of science and medicine, but Moses needed to be able to discuss Jewish studies with
other Jewish scholars. This absence of Jewish scholarship was a
serious disappointment. He began to wonder if a move to the
larger community in Cairo would not be a good idea.

At the same time, the tight-knit community of Alexandria
did not allow one to easily disappear into an ivory tower. The
Jewish community quickly discovered Moses. The most brilliant
and scholarly among them, his opinions were constantly consulted on all matters, private and communal, although officially

he did not hold the title of rabbi. Moses did not really object to either the honor or the extra work; he accepted both with the perfect manners of the Spanish gentleman he never ceased to be. Leadership came as naturally to Moses as scholarship, and despite all the protests in his letters, he enjoyed such leadership.

More and more Moses came to view the Karaites as a major source of trouble. He saw them as catalysts for mixed marriages and some actual conversions, and as having the tendency to admire material possessions over scholarship. Because of the seriousness of the Karaite attack on rabbinic tradition, Moses strongly believed that the Jews ought to separate themselves from the Karaites. At that time, he did not have the power to impose his opinions; only later in life could he put these views into edicts. Nor did he wish to hurt or offend the Karaites. Moses aspired to win them back to rabbinic Judaism. When a Jew asked him how religious Jews should behave toward the Karaites, Moses gave the surprising answer that total isolation from them was not required. A Jew should show the Karaites honor and respect due to any other human being; he should act justly and peacefully toward them and extend services such as circumcision and burial rituals. A Jew could drink their wine and visit them socially, except on days on which the Karaites celebrated holidays at different times from regular Jews, which would desecrate tradition.

However, treating the Karaites with respect did not change the fact that Moses did not consider them true Jews anymore, but a nation apart. In the *Commentary on the Mishna* he stated that they acted against the word of God. He would accept them as Jews only if they returned openly to rabbinic Judaism. A few years later, Moses not only got away with such statements, but won serious victories against the Karaites. But as a young, new scholar in town, his views caused an uproar. The established, powerful wealthy Karaites made it clear that they wanted this young and offensive upstart to leave town. Their dislike started a wave of harassments, which Moses complained about in his letters, though he did not explain the exact nature of the attacks. It is clear, however, that life in Alexandria had become socially and financially difficult for him. Some scholars speculate that the situation brought him close to bankruptcy.

At the same time, within a few short months of their arrival in Alexandria, Rabbi Maimon's health began rapidly to fail. Much as they tried, the family and the doctors could do nothing for him. Rabbi Maimon quietly passed away. His father's death staggered Moses. It didn't matter that he knew how sick and old his father had become toward the end of his life; Rabbi Maimon may have been feeble in body, but never in mind, and to Moses he never stopped being the tower of strength, the guiding light. The little family, deprived of a physical home for so many years, was emotionally dependent on each other to an extent that is hard for us to grasp today. Numerous letters of consolation were received from all over the Jewish world. The passing of that gentle, noble soul was mourned by thousands.

AS THEY BEGAN TO RECOVER the loss of their father, Moses and David had to rethink their financial arrangements; they were on their own for the first time. Moses was thirty-one, and had never had to earn his own living. His friends suggested he apply for a rabbinical position; the community would be happy to pay him a regular salary. Moses adamantly refused to do that. Despite the fact that he enjoyed fulfilling public duties and settling legal matters, he strongly objected to earning a living from the rabbinate and using the Torah as a trade. His strict and unreasonable view was not shared by many others, who did earn a living from the rabbinate and were subsidized entirely by the community. They argued for their point of view. Moses stuck to his own views. He said that the prominent rabbis of the past never received a salary; the great Rabbi Hillel worked as a woodcutter, others worked as merchants, farmers, even blacksmiths. If any of them asked for money, the community would have filled their houses with gold, but they preferred to live independently—and so did he.

At the time, a salaried position was a matter of choice; only two centuries later the community started paying its rabbis on a regular basis. However, the duties of the rabbi were enormously time-consuming. Demanding that, in addition to all his public duties, a rabbi must also pursue a trade for the ten to twelve hours that represented a normal working day at the time, seems unreasonable. Yet this is exactly what Moses demanded of himself and did a little later in life. In addition, he produced a huge body of literature (writing, it must be remembered, every word with a quill pen). The sheer magnitude of his work would have taken other even prodigious thinkers and writers two lifetimes to accomplish—even with the luxury and assistance of our modern-day technology and innovation to speed them along. His productivity cannot be easily explained, and despite the strain, he lived a reasonably long life, by the standard of the era. Later, his son Abraham followed his example and worked as a doctor, a nagid and a writer. He succumbed to the strain however, and overwork killed Abraham at the age of fifty-one.

He could teach, too; however Moses, the quintessential educator, did not really like classroom teaching. He was, above all, a writer, as is obvious not only from his enormous output, but from the fact that he wrote under all conditions and any circumstances. Nothing prevented him from writing. He began writing early and he wrote with a remarkable earnestness and prodigiousness until the end of his life. Occasionally, he acted as a tutor or a mentor for an individual—his brother, his son and some of his disciples. At one point, he gave some series of lectures. His desire to teach, though, was really associated strictly with the written word, and in this sense he was very eager to teach, to transmit and share knowledge. One even wonders if he could have tolerated teaching, as in the classroom, of individuals who were intellectually inferior, even though he strongly criticized teachers who treated any student with condensation or disrespect. Moses could not make up his mind what profession to pursue.

David was a very well-educated man. In a letter, Moses later described him as one who was well versed in the Bible and the Talmud, and a superb grammarian. One can expect no less from a man who was fortunate enough to be educated by Rabbi Maimon and Moses Maimonides. But David liked his profession of gem trading, intended to make a good living and had no desire to live the rabbinic or scholarly life. He devoted some thought to the matter, and suggested to Moses a practical arrangement that would make both of them happy and comfortable. They would pool all the money each had, including the modest sum they inherited from Rabbi Maimon, and invest it together in gems and jewels. David would actively pursue the business, and Moses, as a silent partner, could continue with his studies and community interests, free from the need to earn a living. Moses though, felt David would be working hard, while allowing his big brother to live in what Moses called "carefree indolence." This concern amused David, coming from a man who worked so hard and so selflessly on behalf of the community. Finally, David convinced Moses to see the logic of the arrangement. The partnership worked out extremely well. David was exceptionally clever in his dealings, and the brothers' little capital grew.

But David and Moses both wanted to leave Alexandria and its antagonistic climate. Because of the Karaite scandal, many influential people disliked Moses, and the harassments he experienced began to interfere with his work. A move to the well-established, large community in Fustat, an old and pleasant city near Cairo, and the home of many scholars was discussed. The community there expressed their welcome in advance.

For David's business Fustat would mean tremendous growth opportunities, and he was very much inclined to go there. Local business would be very good; the women of the caliph's court lived in Cairo, and they were probably the best Jewelry customers in Egypt. Many other wealthy citizens lived there as well. For international business, Cairo's position, not far from the Red Sea and right on the Nile, was ideal. Merchants preferred launching their business from the safe Red Sea to the Mediterranean, which was overrun by dangerous Crusader ships.

The women of the Maimon household, though no records remain of their thoughts, were probably delighted to move to the most sophisticated and exciting city in Egypt. Undoubtedly they had relatives and friends there. And this would not be a hasty, furtive move, as fugitives. The family could carefully prepare and pack, get a comfortable house in advance and arrange for the most convenient type of caravan for the benefit of the women and the children. Perhaps, Moses hoped, this would be the last move. Perhaps they could finally settle and live a normal life.

The Fortress of Babylon in Fustat. The use of polychrome masonry, a hallmark of Islamic architecture, was influenced by the ancient building, which was renovated by Emperor Trajan.
(Photo by Mary Knight)

# 7

## New Beginning in Fustat

*A community is like a ship;*
*everyone ought to be prepared to take the helm.*
—*Henrik Ibsen*

CAIRO AND FUSTAT (today known as Old Cairo),[1] two cities of
great importance, stood only two miles apart. Cairo housed the
seat of Egypt's administration, including the caliph's court,
troops, harem and entourage, and a large number of poor people working as menials. Fustat provided a home mostly to the
middle class. Despite being inland cities, not Mediterranean
ports, the two cities together represented the commercial and
financial center of Egypt. Merchants paid customs there for all
the goods they wished to eventually ship from Alexandria, and
could obtain foreign currency only in Cairo and Fustat. They
also stored their goods there, and many commodities that originally came through Alexandria were only available in Cairo and
Fustat. Some surviving letters from Alexandrians complained
that they traveled to Fustat to purchase simple things such as
shoes, clothing, work implements and ink, because they could
buy nothing worthwhile in Alexandria.

Just like Alexandria, Fustat attracted many foreigners. In
Alexandria they consisted of short-term transients, mostly
sailors or traveling merchants; Fustat represented a place they
meant to immigrate to and settle down in, so the city remained
peaceful. It showed little of the clashes between foreigners and

*Above:* Street in Fustat (Old Cairo) and below, architectual features of stone doorways.
(Photos by Mary Knight)

locals that made Alexandria notoriously troublesome. The Jewish community, richer and more comfortably settled, naturally experienced fewer problems with the Muslim authorities than the Alexandrian Jewish community. It also enjoyed special dignity as the seat of the nagid.

The Jews of Fustat led curiously modern and cosmopolitan lives. Most were well traveled, and if they didn't travel much themselves, had large circles of international acquaintance and correspondence, ate exotic foods, wore imported clothes and used artifacts from all over the known world in their homes. Typically middle class, with great interest in commerce and community affairs, they ignored all military affairs, leaving such matters to the court of Cairo. They regarded weapons as tools against bandits, and war as something professionals soldiers waged. Its glory meant nothing to them. They were badgered by a high level of tension and strife, but this was caused by family troubles, professional and financial issues and a tremendous amount of litigation—evils which to our day, are the mark of societies dominated by the middle class. The Jews of Fustat's lifestyle would completely resemble modern society's if it were not for the depth and importance of religion, which played a much larger role in their daily lives and consciousness. Religious and social lives were entirely entwined.

Intensely social people, they disliked being alone or isolated. Visiting and staying over took place mostly on Saturdays, but even during week days they regularly socialized, mostly with people of the same gender. They cared about what other people said about them—and indulged in tremendous amounts of gossip. Everyone minded everybody else's business, both personal and professional; some people even set themselves up officially to correct other people's bad behavior. However, they considered compassion to be the most important trait of character any man or woman could exhibit.

The most elevated person in the community was the scholar. It did not matter much what the he did for a living; even if the man performed manual, poorly paid-for labor, his scholarly mind was utterly respected. Religion encouraged such opinions. S.D. Goitein, one of the greatest experts on the era, explained that rabbinical Judaism was a religion for scholarly minds. Only a scholar, for example, could be the leader of the community—even the richest man, or the descendant of the most noble family would not be accepted if he were not a scholar. Surprisingly, despite such encouragement for study, the Egyptian Jewish community did not have as many scholars as Spain did during the Golden Age.

The presence of many Christians in Fustat tempted many Muslims to relax their objection to wine drinking, and encouraged the Jews to pursue their passion for secular music and recitation of lighthearted poetry. Both Muslim and Jewish authorities objected to these deviations from the straight and narrow path, but the inhabitants continued to do exactly as they pleased. Moses disapproved. He would not have minded the poetry, which he remembered as a part of life in Spain, but even that displeased him because the poetry was not as good or as sophisticated as the poetry composed by the Jews of Spain. He objected to dice games on Saturday, which the Jews loved to play, along with much drinking and socializing. Later, when he took over the leadership of the Jewish community, he allowed only non-gambling games on Saturdays.

Wine presented a complicated social issue. The Law considered wine sacramental, and therefore only Jews were permitted to drink it together. Many of the Jews of Fustat had Muslim friends, and they wanted to be able to share wine with them. Surprisingly, Moses solved this problem. First, he knew that friendly relations between Jews and Muslims was a good social habit. Second, he did not really object to moderate wine drinking, although drunkenness repelled him. He ruled that dropping a small quantity of honey into the wine—because honey was not permitted in the old Temple services—turned it from a sacramental beverage into a soft drink. The benediction the Jews were required to say over the mixture was the same one said over water and soft drinks, not over wine, therefor Muslim and Jewish friends could socialize and enjoy the pleasure of drinking wine together.

Music was highly popular in Fustat and when Moses first arrived in the city, he was surprised by such extensive activity, because it often involved mingling with women—as singers and players of the instruments—who provided the music. Traditional Jewish law generally objected to music, at least in theory. Moses' attitude was ambivalent. In his responsa to scholars, he explained the value music could have as an aid to spiritual experience. But for the masses, he continued to object to it throughout his career—without much success. The Jews of Fustat loved music, and little could be done about it.

Altogether, Fustat was a stimulating and lively city, and even with its drawbacks, a very hospitable place to settle. It was unofficially zoned into residential and commercial areas, with certain trades functioning in dedicated streets. No one enforced such divisions. Some stores functioned in largely residential areas, and were owned by the residents. Also, many multiple-story houses existed in the commercial zones. The upper stories were often used as residential apartments by store owners who operated their business from the street level. These arrangements depended on economic levels—the more affluent preferred to live in elegant, all-residential areas, the less affluent combined the two formats.

Jews lived in concentrated neighborhoods that allowed close proximity to the synagogue, because travel under Jewish law was forbidden on Saturday. The authorities did not restrict them to these areas, and often their neighborhoods included Muslims and Christians. However, Jews generally disliked living in the same house with Muslims, because Jewish women were much less restricted in their movements than Muslim women, and they were inconvenienced by the Muslim women's habits. The decision on where the family lived usually stayed with the woman as a right specified in the marriage contract.

Strangely, in this bustling and prosperous city, many neglected buildings fell into decay and stood as ruins, side by side with beautiful, well-kept homes. Regulations for the upkeep of houses did not exist, and many neighborhoods suffered from this situation. Apparently, the respect for the individual's right to do what he or she pleased with personal property was stronger than the dislike of looking at such neglected sites.

Busy semi-public houses served as banks, places for public notaries and offices of great merchants (they were called "houses," though they looked more like bazaars). Much of the jewelry trade took place in the Jewelry House, where David probably visited regularly. Money was changed and credit established in the House of Blessings, or in the House of Money Changing, a place that became so famous that one could send a letter to this establishment without writing the address. Not too far stood the Mint, which employed many people. Numerous hotels and caravanserai received the constant stream of travelers.

The synagogue functioned as the Jewish center of life. Not only was it a place of worship, but it also served as a center for communal affairs, a library, a hospice for travelers, a center of judicial authority and the most important center of study. Aside from these extra activities, the long services were held three times a day and required strict attendance. One could not decide to attend only on the Sabbath. People never missed the Monday and Thursday sessions, in which the Torah scrolls were taken out and read, and important matters requiring oaths were discussed in front of the open ark. Many enjoyed the *piyyutim*,[2] which were long and time-consuming and extended the service considerably. The people did not see the time they spent in the synagogue as a chore, but rather as a vibrant aspect of their community and spiritual lives.

The citizens of Fustat loved comfort and luxury, and accordingly, their houses were as beautiful and as comfortably built and furnished as possible. The actual location of the house where the Maimon family settled in Fustat is debated, but most houses of middle-class families had much in common, and the household of Moses' family can be assumed to follow a certain pattern.

Most homes, even the modest ones, were made up of a few

floors. Houses were built in such a way as to allow expansion, so that families could stay together as they grew, or use for renting purposes. A house had at least one entrance, usually more, with decorative doors equipped with a knocker ring, and a bay window located strategically above it, where the inhabitants could sit on a small balcony. Many other windows allowed ample light into the house. We can assume that an extended family such as the Maimons had a large communal living room on the ground floor with a few adjoining small rooms, a few apartments on two upper floors, a logia[3] and an inner court. The upper floors would each have included a large living room and a few smaller rooms attached. Wash rooms were built inside. Good storage rooms, both open to the air and in cellars were essential. Stables to shelter the donkeys and mules were useful, but often people rented their animals rather than owned them, so they did not exist in all households.

The houses were designed to be as roomy as possible; the architectural ideal was the introduction of God's expanse of sky into the house. To achieve that, an inner court, often including a garden and a fountain and open to the sky, was constructed so that it was part of the interior. The living room was always spacious, but bedrooms were small. It was easier to sleep in tiny, easily heated bedrooms in winter, and in the living room itself in the summer, where a special ventilation shaft kept it cool.[4] Therefore, most of the ground floor of the house was devoted to the living room. In it, structural elements such as recesses and niches replaced heavy armoires. There was no need for large tables, since the food was brought in and eaten wherever one wished, on movable trays. Upholstered benches lined the walls, and small movable pieces of furniture allowed visual spaciousness. For storage, they used boxes, trunks and chests, sometimes highly ornamental. Baskets of different materials, beautifully woven and covered with palm fronds, held housewares, tableware and even food. Most of these containers were covered with embroidered fabrics and with laces.

Tables, chairs and beds as we know them were not used, other than the upholstered benches. Instead, a wonderful array of gorgeous fabrics of all colors, shapes and designs was spread on the floor—carpeting, mattresses, pillows, bolsters, cushions and sofa cushions to recline on and pillows to sleep on. One special furnishing often mentioned in descriptions of wealthy homes consisted of two parts: a seat itself and a back support, made of heavy silk shot with gold threads. Beds were piled with many layers of mattresses and pads, and often topped with colorful canopies. Curtains did not cover the windows—which would prevent ventilation—but served between rooms instead of doors, in front of the wall recesses, as room dividers to be used when wanted and to line the walls. Light wooden shutters provided the windows with privacy, when needed. Carpets and wall hangings also hung on walls, allowing an air of opulence even in middle-class homes.

At night, houses were brightly illuminated. Officially for nightly studies, unofficially for parties; the citizens of Fustat did not go to bed early. They used oil lamps of various materials and shapes, and suspended chandeliers and candlesticks for the very expensive wax candles, if the household could afford them. In the street, they carried lanterns. They also had fumigation devices, and burned aromatic woods in braziers and censers made of copper, bronze and silver. Fumigation was needed to clear the house of unpleasant odors, and for freshening it after each meal, but the custom, together with sprinkling with rose water, also served as a pleasure in itself, much like smoking or wearing perfumes.

EGYPT WAS A HAVEN from harrassment and persecution. Enjoying the easier lifestyle, Moses settled to work happily in Fustat. As usual, he immediately became involved in community affairs, but mostly he concentrated on finishing his *Commentary on the Mishna,* or the *Siraj,* which he had started in Spain and worked on throughout the years of wandering. Working under such pleasant conditions in a nice home, with his family safe and comfortable, and surrounded by the peaceful atmosphere of the tolerant and well-mannered community felt like an unusual luxury.

Moses had an inner sense that in this sanctuary he would spend the rest of his life. He would never love Egypt as he had loved Spain; nor would he idolize it as he did Palestine. He would never sign his name as "Moses of Egypt," only as "Moses the Spaniard," and would always maintain a wistful note when writing, often referring to "at home in Andaluse . . ." But he knew Egypt would become his adopted country—and they would serve each other well.

Some of the legends claim Moses lived in dire poverty until the sultan was to make him a favorite, but this is merely a myth, intended to show how perfectly Moses believed in God under any conditions. In truth, while the family may not have been rich, they certainly were reasonably well off. They lived comfortably in a nice house, ate good food, dressed very well and could even afford some luxuries, widely available in Fustat.

Food in Fustat was good and varied. Muslims and Jews shared similar cuisines except for the specialties, such as the particular foods that had to be prepared for the Sabbath, when Jews were forbidden to cook. Muslims loved these specialties, and were often entertained in the homes of their Jewish friends. Some of the delicacies included chicken in lemon sauce, and fat tail of sheep. The more fat in the food, the better. They loved vegetables, cooked in various ways and adored sweets made from honey, raisins and dates. People took their food seriously and physicians wrote treatises about the health of various foodstuffs, and cookbooks of various levels of complexity were available to cooks. In later life, Moses was often asked about the virtues or evils of certain foodstuffs. He highly recommended honey made of good, fresh dates, mixed with water and served with bread, as quick energy food for the scholar. Another food Moses recommended, which remained in Jewish folklore as the ideal food, were mixed almonds and raisins, taken with bread. This particular dish crossed the continents and the centuries. Some Yiddish songs from nineteenth-century Eastern Europe celebrate its virtues.

People ate two meals per day. A light morning meal, taken after prayer and perhaps a few hours of work, and a substantial evening meal. For this evening meal, people ate a few courses, though fewer than in the West. On Saturday, Jews ate three meals. Despite their appreciation of food, people ate moderately and considered obesity or gluttony inappropriate. The pleasant odors of cooked foods permeated Fustat, with large quantities of prepared foods always available at the bazaars. Most working people bought their morning meal every day, but often people bought dinner as well, to save themselves the trouble of having to cook in the evening.

The variety of foods available to individuals depended on the wealth of the family. Surviving household accounts show that common ingredients included olive oil, cream, honey and assorted domestic and imported cheeses. People ate fish and various meats such as beef, chicken and mutton and local vegetables such as cucumbers, parsley, asparagus, garlic, onions and radishes. Legumes included chickpeas, lentils and beans. Local fruit included apples, oranges, bananas, figs, grapes and watermelon, with dried apricots, plums and peaches being imported. Many spices were used, showing that the variety of prepared foods was large, including coriander, rose water and saffron. They also imported various nuts and almonds, made them into sweets, and used fruit and sugar to make candy.

People considered bread to be the most important food, and used mostly wheat for their baking. They bought the wheat as grain, had it ground at a local mill, prepared the dough at home and had the bread baked at a local bakery. Grain was sometimes difficult to come by and the fluctuations of the market occasionally caused the prices to soar, so buying large quantities of wheat at harvest time and storing it for the winter was a common habit.

Both the Muslims and Jews of Fustat were attentive to their physical appearance, grooming, jewelry and clothes. Those who dealt professionally with clothes were highly respected, and scholars considered the clothing industry a most suitable way to support themselves. It is interesting to note that the food industry, on the other hand, was handled by people of low rank or by women, whose status depended on their husbands'. People were less willing to spend the great deals of money on food that they did on clothes.

The objection of the religious authorities to luxurious clothes, strong during biblical times, all but disappeared in Egypt during the High Middle Ages, though it survived in the Maghreb. Men were encouraged to spend freely on their children's and wives' clothing, and when the community distributed clothes to the poor, women's needs took precedence over men's.

Everyone wore several layers of clothing, and Jewish men wore the *tallith* as outwear. Today the tallith, or prayer shawl, is worn only during prayer. Then, Jewish men used it as the upper garment, with the biblically proscribed fringed or tassled corners, as a reminder of their bond and duty to God. Later, because of public humiliations the rabbis limited its wear to the synagogue or at home, during prayer services.

Men's robes were designed so that no part of their body should be seen under it. The man girded his robe with a belt, and then wrapped himself in the tallith. Underneath the tallith, the robe was not supposed to show more than a handbreadth. Finally, he put on his shoes, since they were never worn indoors, only outside. The body was further covered by wide, long sleeves, blending the arms with the body. The sleeves served as pockets. A man used a special sleeve kerchief to tie small possessions in, tucked it into his sleeve—and lost it quite often. A universal decoration for both men and women was the sleeve band. On the upper part of the sleeve was a stripe of different color, often embroidered with a script, a verse or some other decoration. Sleeves could be purchased separately, unattached to the garment.

Male and female clothes were not entirely different in cut, the main idea being to conceal the shape of the body. Modesty was essential, nakedness considered a sin, so the shape of the body and limbs had to be disguised. Shape and ornamentation were different between the genders, but in a poor household, man and wife often shared an outer robe. Both men and women divided their wardrobe into holiday clothes and working day clothes. The holiday clothes included a different headgear.

Ordinary workers sometimes neglected their working wardrobes, but businessmen had to be well dressed during the week, to create the right impression. At night, people changed for sleeping, but the shape of the sleeping clothes was much like those worn during the day.

Turbans were the most important part of a man's outfit. The turban was costly, and its size and value showed the wearer's position in society. The wimple, worn by women, served the same purpose. Wearing headgear was also a sign of respect for God. In his writings, Moses recommended following the example of the talmudic sage who declared that he never walked bareheaded even for a short distance, because God's presence always hovered over his head.

Shoes presented an amusing dilemma. On one hand, people considered shoes "unmentionable," possibly because of their association with the dirt in the street. On the other hand, they loved owning beautiful shoes of various shapes and colors and even had a custom dictating that a bridegroom send a present of shoes to his bride and all her female relatives—but not talk about it. Other "unmentionables" were the underpants, which were worn by everyone, but regular trousers were not used.

Linen, widely cultivated and indigenous to the area, served as the most popular fabric since the days of the Pharaohs. Cotton, while still imported from India, was less widely used, but when the peasants started cultivating it in Egypt, it became cheap enough for the poor. Wool was not very popular, but silk arriving from China, though it remained an item of luxury, was in high demand. The dyeing industries and their brilliant colors were also well-developed during Moses' days. The purple dye made from shellfish and mentioned in the Bible was originally used only for royalty. During the twelfth century this ruling no longer existed, and purple dye was used extensively. Clothes were colored indigo, bright saffron yellow, crimson, bright blue, light sky blue, green and white, with each color possessing a bewildering and sophisticated array of shades. Whites, for example, could be "snow colored," "pearl colored," "cloud colored," "white asparagus colored," "glass colored" or "crystal colored. Black was worn extensively as a ceremonial, festive and mourning color. To add to the color and fashion interest, much embroidery was used. It was not only the time-honored leisure occupation of many women in their homes, but an entire industry was devoted to it. The well-developed fashion and clothing industry allowed people to buy many of their clothes ready-made, with perhaps some adjustments made at home. The washing and starching was done mostly by professionals outside the home.

WITH SUCH FINE and sophisticated appreciation of beauty, it is no wonder that David's business flourished in Fustat. Jewelry appeared as a major item in all the Geniza trousseau lists, showing that most women had at least some precious jewelry; the well-to-do owned extensive collections. Traders such as David, aided by the well-developed Islamic science, knew a great deal about the properties of precious stones.

Much of the Jewelry consisted of heavy gold. Some bracelets weighted as much as a full pound. Women wore bracelets, anklets, earrings, necklaces, pins and rings. Various designs had interesting trade names such as "Scorpion's Venom" and "Breast of the Falcon," as well as modern terms such as "Solitaire." Gold was fashioned in many shapes and forms, such as birds, fruit, flowers, crescents, sun disks and filigree. Pearls featured as second in popularity to gold, and played a large part in David's business. The traders imported vast quantities from India, and an entire industry of perforating and stringing developed in Egypt. Middle-class Jewish women rarely acquired the true precious stones—rubies, emeralds, sapphires and diamonds. Very wealthy men owned those, usually set as signet rings, and considered them suitable gifts for dignitaries. Since David traded with Muslims as well as with Jews, he dealt regularly with these costly items.

Many middle-class women also wore costume jewelry and semi-precious stones, often ornamental and artistically shaped. These included coral, cowry shells, various types of beads, amber, carnelians, lapis lazuli and even fragrant cloves set in chains. These women also wore ornaments made of bronze and brass, then gilded with gold. Silver played a minor part in jewelry, though often it was used for vessels in the home and for many ritual objects.

David's business developed swiftly, but if he wanted to achieve real success he would need to travel extensively, as commerce during the twelfth century was an international affair. Moses did not want to see him leave Fustat. David had not as yet made long distance voyages, but even the little trips he took across Egypt caused Moses to worry incessantly about the safety of the man he still viewed as his little brother. His anxiety became so intense, that whenever David left, Moses fasted, and when he came back, Moses contributed to charity as thanksgiving. He vigorously attempted to dissuade David from long distant travel, and most vehemently objected to sea travel, still recalling the horrible experience of their trip to Palestine.

His brother did not wish to cause Moses pain and anxiety, but he knew there was no choice in the matter. They had long discussions; finally David persuaded Moses to see reason. A merchant could not shirk the responsibility of travel, he said. No commercial house dealing with gems and jewels could prosper, or even survive, without it. God would undoubtedly guard him and return him safely to his family. Reluctantly, Moses gave in. David's first long trip was meant to be by land only. One autographed letter he sent to Moses from the Sudanese port city, Aydhab, survives in the Cairo Geniza. This detailed and interesting letter shows the great love between the brothers.

David was lucky to be alive and in Aydhab at all. The trip started well; David and a few other merchants left Fustat with a caravan heading for Qus, a city on the Nile in Upper Egypt. They planned to rest there, replenish their supplies and then continue on the seventeen-day trip to Aydhab. Because of the dangers of the desert—thirst, sand storms, losing one's way and extremely dangerous gangs of robbers—everyone regarded a caravan with a large number of people as the only way to travel.

Somehow David and one other companion were separated

from the caravan in Qus. He does not explain in his letter how it happened, and we may never know what caused the separation. We do know that the two of them decided to cross the desert to Aydhab by themselves, an act of sheer folly. Even David, this most adventurous soul, admitted in the letter that this was a foolhardy idea. His only justification for attempting it was, he said, that he was ignorant of the danger, that he was stupid. It's hard to believe that an intelligent and experienced traveler like David did not know about the dangers of traveling alone across the desert.

The two companions crossed the desert, but we will never know about their adventures because David flatly refused to give any details. He wrote Moses that he did not wish to distress him by repeating all the frightening hardships they had to undergo. They reached their destination in a state of exhaustion, but unhurt and with all their goods intact. Ironically, the caravan they originally separated from arrived at the same time. They did not fare so well. Robbers attacked them in the desert, took all their goods and wounded some of them. A few died on their way, suffering from their wounds and from thirst.

In the meantime, trying to keep track of David, Moses heard about the attack on the original caravan. He had no idea that David and his companion had struck out on their own, and assumed that he was hurt, perhaps dead; and the suspense tormented him. Fortunately, when arriving in Aydhab, David heard about his brother's attempts to reach him, and as quickly as possible sent a letter to reassure Moses that all was well, and that his own stupidity saved him. Or more likely, he said, it was the will of God.

He used his idea of God's protection to reconcile Moses to the next part of the adventure. Looking about them in Aydhab, David and his companion were disappointed. They could only purchase indigo, a useless substance for both of them. The companion immediately arranged a sea voyage to India for himself, and left. David, frustrated and annoyed, decided to do the same despite his promise to Moses not to take a sea voyage. He reassured Moses again and again that God, who saved him in the desert, would do so at sea as well.

His original companions from the robbed caravan also went to India. It's difficult to understand how they managed this, having been robbed of all their goods and money, but perhaps they had credit established in Aydhab. Many merchants had such affiliations in all commercial centers, and Jews in particular had excellent credit systems established since the early Middle Ages. Apparently, Moses knew these merchants, because David mentions their names in his letter to Moses, perhaps as another way to reassure Moses that his brother was safe and in good company.

David also asked Moses to calm the heart of his wife, to whom he refers as "the little one," a title reserved for a young wife who had not yet become "the great one," the matriarchal grandmother she would some day be. He greeted his wife's sister, who lived with them in this extended family,[5] and sent his regards to the rest of the household as well, including all the children, and to one liberated slave who apparently lived with the extended family. He sent good wishes to his brother-in-law and to all his friends. These messages were completely informal, genuine and heartfelt, and they break the taboo against mentioning women in a letter and sending them direct messages. Reading David's letter, the eight-hundred-year-old gulf between his time and our own seems to be bridged; David possessed an entirely modern mind.

By the time Moses got the letter, David's boat had already sailed to India. He mentioned that he would leave in the middle of the month of Ramadan, a holy Muslim holiday. The middle of Ramadan had passed when Moses held the letter in his hands, worrying and debating how to tell the difficult news to the rest of the family. The younger brother had made his own decision without the permission of his older brother. Moses accepted the situation, and as usual, fasted and prayed. David came back safely from his first big, extremely prosperous trip, and was flush with success and adventure. There would be future trips, and Moses knew it.

# 8

## A Luminous Light: *The Siraj*

Look then, into thine heart, and write!
—*Henry Wadsworth Longfellow*

THE YEAR 1168 marked the completion of Moses Maimonides' first major work—the *Siraj*, or the *Commentary on the Mishna*. In the *Siraj*, Maimonides followed his life-long ideal—bringing order and system into the immense body of Jewish law, presenting it in clear form and making it accessible to all who want to pursue it. The magnitude of the task defies the imagination, and yet, to a large extent, Maimonides accomplished it.

The Mishna, the codified core of the Oral Law, preceeds the Talmud in point of time, but it gradually became subservient to and assimilated in the Talmud as a unit of study. In the introduction to his book *A Maimonides Reader*, Isadore Twersky explains that while several commentaries on the Talmud existed during Maimonides' time, commentaries on the Mishna "were rare and fragmentary." In an effort to rehabilitate the Mishna "as a complete self-sufficient unit of study," Twersky says, Maimonides intended his commentary to serve both as

> an *introduction* to the Talmud—this follows from the nature of the Mishna–and as a *review* of the Talmud—this follows from the nature of his commentary which summarizes different interpretations and indicates the normative conclusions.

81

The Oral Law includes all Jewish law that is not explicitly set forth in the Written Law, or the Scriptures, and traditional Judaism considers them both as equally authoritative. The Mishna, the first rabbinical text and the core document of talmudic tradition, began with Rabbi Akiva ben Joseph after the Bar-Cochba revolt, was continued by Rabbi Akiva's disciples—primarily Rabbi Meir—and was completed in the early part of the third century by Rabbi Judah ha-Nasi, Maimonides' ancestor.

The Mishna is divided into six orders, each order is divided into tractates and each tractate is divided into chapters, according to subject matter. The chapters consist of individual "mishnas" or paragraphs. The Mishna was meant to be a code of Jewish law, but it is much more than that. It contains many disputes, minority opinions and nonlegal materials. The language is terse, often a solution is missing and it requires interpretation and clarification. The Talmud was supposed to fill the gap, but was often too obscure, incomplete or unintelligible. Also, the Talmud contained new material not mentioned in the Mishna at all, as it was developed much later.

Maimonides set out to correct these problems. The *Siraj* makes it possible to make decisions without complicated talmudic research. It was not only useful to the layman or a beginning student, even a talmudic scholar could benefit from studying it, since it removed the obscurities and problems from many complicated Mishna passages and explained them properly. Furthermore, after each explanation, Maimonides states how the practical decision was determined. To make matters even clearer, he often omits a discussion of the views of those whose decision was not accepted as final, and so avoided the subtle and confusing discussions which dominated the Talmud. Sometimes he stated his own views as the correct ones—against the authority of the Talmud. He often did not cite works of his predecessors, but instead claimed in the introduction that he gave them credit for all he learned from them. He also used the principles of other sciences to show how he came to various conclusions; this innovation shocked some conservative readers.

*Above:* Inner entrance to
A1-Azhar University in Cairo.
This is the foremost center of
theology in Islam and very likely
the oldest university in the world.

*Right:* The doorway to the library
at Al-Azhar University.

(Photos by Mary Knight)

A few subjects he discusses reveal interesting character points. One of them is the question of the *Olam Haba*. This term can be directly translated as "The Next World," and it deals with the subject of life after death. The Mishna states, "All Israelites have a share in the Olam Haba." In his interpretation, Maimonides claimed that many Jews formed the wrong idea of what the "next world" actually meant.

Some believed in the literalness of heaven and hell. To these believers, heaven represented physical comforts, rivers of milk and honey, lovely clothes and beautiful homes. In hell, the wicked would be tortured and burned. A second group, believers in the messianic tradition, expected to be transformed into gigantic angel-like beings, immortal and happy, and well provided with food and clothes. The wicked, these believers maintained, would not participate in the Messianic Age. A third group believed that the righteous would be resurrected, live happily with their families and never die again. The wicked would not be resurrected. A fourth group believed that following the Law would give them earthly rewards such as money, beautiful homes, many children and good health. The Jews would have their own kingdom, where they would rule over all those who hurt them in the past. The wicked would continue to suffer. Finally, there were those who combined all these beliefs, and imagined all sorts of earthly delights after the arrival of the Messiah.

Maimonides further divided the Jews into three groups, based upon their intellectual capacity. The first group took the words of the sages' discussion of the Olam Haba, or the Torah Nistara, the Hidden Torah, literally, and did not see the hidden meanings. This group was culturally and intellectually underdeveloped, and Maimonides saw them as destroying the glory of the Law by their ignorance. The second group also took the sages' words literally, but condemned them and ridiculed them without attempting to grasp the hidden meaning. They were, if anything, worse than the first group. The third group Maimonides defined as the few and select who understood the allegorical nature of what the sages had to say about the Olam Haba.

Like a teacher rewarding a child for studying, the sages tried to impress rewards on the common man for following the Law. But as the child outgrows the need for rewards and begins to like his studies for their own sake, at some point the wise man begins to follow the Law for its own sake.

To the wise man, Olam Haba is not a place of physical rewards, but of divine glory. Perhaps paradise is a place of beauty, perhaps hell is a place of torture, but either way it matters very little, and no sage specified precisely what the joys or suffering actually would be. The important goal any thinking man wanted to achieve was the enlightened state in which God's existence is understood. When life brings sorrow and trouble, most human beings want to be acknowledged, comforted, rewarded. Maimonides, who unquestionably lived a life of great difficulties and sorrows, asked for no physical reward. The only joy he sought was the perfect knowledge of God. Maimonides dwelled, spiritually, in a rarefied atmosphere.

His thoughts regarding the Messianic Age are also significant. It meant to him the return of the Jews to Palestine and the creation of their own kingdom—and without the slightest supernatural overtone. The king/Messiah would neither bring an unnatural utopia, nor would he be immortal. He would be a mortal man and his descendants would rule after him. The life span of most people would be extended because of their righteous lifestyle, but people would not necessarily own better homes, or ride stronger animals or wear more beautiful clothes. People would not even reach equality among themselves. Inequality would continue to exist between rich and poor, master and servant, man and woman. But the ownership of the land would allow Jews to pursue the Torah peacefully. This view naturally was not popular with many people who expected magical messianic times.

Another interesting segment of the *Siraj* is the Thirteen Articles: a set of articles of faith that every Jew must hold to share in the Olam Haba; if even one is denied, so says the *Siraj*, the person will not share in it. Later, these articles were incorporated into the synagogue ritual, but they also incurred a bit of a scandal. People thought it presumptions of Maimonides to determine, on his own, who had a share in the Olam Haba and who did not. No central authority ever held such views, and many rabbis did not agree with these articles.

The Thirteen Articles grew into fundamental principals of Judaism. The individual must believe:

1) in the existence of God; 2) in the unity of God; 3) in the incorporeality of God; 4) in the eternity of God; 5) that all worship and adoration are due to God only; 6) in prophecy; 7) that the biblical Moses was the greatest of prophets; 8) that the Law was given to Moses at Sinai; 9) in the immutability of the Law; 10) that God knows the acts of man; 11) in reward and punishment; 12) in the coming of the Messiah; 13) in the resurrection of the dead.

A fascinating feature of the *Siraj* includes a treatise on psychology and ethics, known as the Eight Chapters. It heavily relies on Aristotelian philosophy, combined with the teachings of the sages. In the first two chapters, the teacher is compared to the physician. Just as the physician must know the body to be able to cure it, so the spiritual teacher must know the soul and so be able to prevent spiritual disease. The third and fourth chapters deal with specific diseases of the soul, and how to balance life without going to extremes (this part is particularly Aristotelian). The fifth chapter, related more closely to the views of the Jewish sages, describes how the aim of life is to understand God. Chapter six is a reconciliation between Greek and Jewish philosophy, regarding perfection in man. Chapter seven discusses prophecy and chapter eight deals with providence and the dangers of astrology.

Maimonides strongly expresses his own views in the *Siraj* on many varied subjects. He condemned various old customs and espoused the need to change them. He declared that scholarship is more important than earthly riches, and scholars should be given special privileges, but at the same time should not make a living from their scholarship. He stormed against astrology and the use of magical amulets. He even contested the opinion of the geonim (the collective head of the rabbinic college or academy), declaring often that though they have decided a certain question, he was of a different opinion.

Often he makes it clear to the reader that he wrote a certain portion in Palestine, another in Egypt, a third one on the road. He tells when he derived something from his father's interpretation. In the epilogue he even talks about himself. He tells the reader about the hardships he had to undergo while working on the book: the general miseries of the time, the exile forced upon him, the constant expulsions and wanderings all over the known world. Perhaps, he wondered, this exile would atone for his sins. He mentions having to write while traveling by land and sea, and explains that while working on this task, he also spent time pursuing other sciences. He welcomed criticism, which he felt was a good deed rewarded by heaven. All in all, he expressed a humble request for acceptance and understanding.

However, not all his statements show humility. He tells the reader to read the book over and over and reflect on it carefully. If the reader felt he understood the book after one—or even ten readings—he was misled by his own foolishness. This book, Maimonides concluded, was written after long research and reflection. (Not too many authors would have had the temerity to command the reader to pursue his book more than ten times.) Maimonides may have aspired to humility with a sincere heart, and had been highly praised for it, but he never lost sight of his own intellectual superiority.

Strangely, the book, which is now an acknowledged masterpiece, did not elicit great interest at the time of its publication. Maimonides felt strongly about restoring the Mishna to its former position of great importance. He believed that even some talmudic scholars did not value the Mishna for itself sufficiently. Perhaps not enough people shared his views.

But despite the criticism, no one was really offended by the book. His contemporaries appreciated the scholarship that went into it, and the respect given to Maimonides increased in intellectual circles. However, it did not make him famous. Benjamin of Tudela, who visited Fustat around the time of the book's publication, always made sure to meet all the Jewish celebrities. He never heard about Maimonides or about the new book. The *Siraj* did strengthen the position Maimonides held within the community though. Still a young man, only in his early thirties, he was already functioning unofficially as a leading citizen of the Jewish community. The book's reputation increased the number of the legal questions addressed to him, and his responsa were already highly valued by their recipients. Most important, the timing of these events was quite fortunate; very soon after the book became available to the public the entire city of Fustat went up in flames.

Outside view of the mosque at Al-Azhar University in Cairo.
(Photo by Mary Knight)

# 9

## The Ascent of Saladin

Every time a conqueror has appeared there have been wars, but this does not
prove that the conquerors caused the wars, or that it is possible to discover
the laws of war in the personal activity of a single man.

—*Count Leo Tolstoy*

THE POLITICAL SITUATION in Egypt grew increasingly volatile.
Several historical versions of the situation debate the exact inter-
change between the principal players, but the core of the story
is simple. Several enemies threatened the weak and ineffective
caliph, El Adid, who showed few marks of distinction and is
remembered mostly because he was the last of the Fatimids. To
defend himself from the powerful Seljuks, he paid a regular tribute to Amalric, the Christian king of Jerusalem, who acted as his
protector. In September 1168, he decided to stop paying the
tribute. Amalric did not wait long to retaliate; in October, he
marched into Egypt, expecting the invasion to provide excellent
opportunities for looting. He accomplished this aim quite successfully on his way to Cairo and Fustat, and in addition, committed atrocities in the town of Bilbay, where a full-scale
massacre was recorded by eyewitnesses.

The heavily fortified Cairo could prepare itself efficiently for
war, but Fustat, an open city, had no means of defense. Losing
Fustat to Amalric would have meant a vital strategic loss, since
the city occupied a key position in upper Egypt. Something had
to be done quickly, before Amalric arrived.

The vizier Shawar, who ruled Egypt for the ineffective

Entrance to the Mosque of
A1-Hakim in Cairo. The mosque
was built during the Fatimid period
and shows strong influence from
North Africa, where the dynasty
originated.

*Below:* Sabil-Kuttab of Abd al-Rah-
man Katkhuda in Cairo. This monument, and the street it stands on, date
back to the Fatimid period.

(Photos by Mary Knight)

caliph, ordered the entire population of Fustat to evacuate the city immediately and take refuge in Cairo. The command, sudden and unexpected, startled the population of Fustat. No one had time to properly prepare for evacuation. Many did not have enough animals ready to carry their possessions and few had access to carts, so they could take with them only the objects they could carry. A great number of the people escaped with very little but the clothes on their backs.

We have no record of how much Maimonides and his brother managed to salvage, but since their money was invested in jewelry and gems, it is likely that they managed to save quite a bit. The two brothers, logical, level-headed and accustomed to fleeing their home in a hurry, probably did not panic. Other people, however, certainly did. They were not sure when the vizier would start to execute his plan, and had no clear idea of what he planned to do in the first place. The uncertainty and fear caused a hasty, disorganized and to some, devastating evacuation. An eyewitness described a scene of total chaos—families separated from each other, people screaming and running—others, even at the last moment, trying to buy or steal any riding animal they could get their hands on. Some people were badly hurt, a few were killed. Eventually Fustat was totally deserted.

On November 22, the slaves of the vizier walked into the silent streets of Fustat. They poured twenty thousand bottles of petroleum over the empty city, and lit ten thousand fuses. A monstrous bonfire that could not be extinguished greeted Amalric and his troops. Fustat burned for two full months.

Amalric was not to be intimidated. He camped by Cairo, and waited for the opportunity to attack. But the tactic gave Shawar some time, and he used it to get in touch with Nurredin of Syria, as the Sultan was commonly known. He implored Nurredin to help his Muslim brothers against the Christian invader. Nurredin could not refuse. He sent his truly superior troops, headed by an experienced commander—his trusted vizier Sherkuh. The commander's nephew, Saladin, accompanied him to Cairo. The young nephew did not greatly distinguish himself in the court of Nurredin, but his friends considered him shrewd and practical. Saladin was not particularly anxious to go to Egypt, but decided to go anyway, to please his uncle. When Amalric heard about Nurredin's involvemnet and the advancing troops, he hastily retreated, knowing full well they would defeat him. However, he took a large number of captives with him, including many Jews.

Sherkuh took charge of the city, and kept his nephew with him to assist in governing and rebuilding it. Saladin proved to be extremely intelligent and skillful, and the inhabitants of Cairo and refugees from Fustat liked both men. The speed and efficiency Saladin showed in his efforts to rebuild Fustat greatly impressed them, and they were delighted with the permission to come back to their city so quickly.

The vizier Shawar, however, resented losing the command of the city to Sherkuh and Saladin, and started plotting against the newcomers. Saladin, who had spies everywhere, quickly learned about the plot and reported it to Sherkuh. After a short consultation, the two decided to arrest Shawar. This act might have been considered an insult to the caliph El Adid, but they shrewdly guessed that El Adid secretly hated and feared his aggressive vizier. To avert any misunderstanding, they reported their plans to El Adid immediately. The caliph, as delighted with this new development as Saladin and Sherkuh expected, requested a gruesome gift—the head of Shawar. The wish was politely granted, and the caliph appointed Sherkuh not only as his new vizier, but as the commander-in-chief of his army. Saladin continued to assist his uncle until March 1169, when Sherkuh suddenly died.

Following Sherkuh's death, El Adid immediately appointed Saladin as the new vizier. Saladin rose steadily in power. The few obstacles that arose he speedily resolved. He crushed a Sudanese rebellion and a plan was needed to deal later with the Crusaders, but once these two issues were settled, all he had to do to reach absolute power was to depose El Adid. Conveniently enough, El Adid was so ill at that time he did not even know that his crown was lost. The change of government took place peacefully in 1171, and from then on Saladin's rule was secure until his death in 1193.

DURING THE REBUILDING, inflation, high prices and a few bouts with plagues made life difficult, but this situation did not last long, and Fustat emerged into a period of strong economic growth. David expanded the business, traveled widely and sailed a few more times to India. Every time he came back safely, Maimonides prayed and fasted in thanks. He no longer tried to prevent David from traveling, but could not reconcile himself to the dangers David put himself through. He would have been quite happy to earn a lot less money and run a smaller business, if his brother only stayed safely home. David, however, felt his business responsibilities required travel, particularly since his wife had given birth to a little daughter. They hoped for more children, and perhaps to see Maimonides marry and have children of his own, for whom the business would also have to provide.

At this point, Maimonides had started an important campaign to release the captive Jews. Tirelessly, he wrote letter after letter to all the communities in Egypt and many outside it, trying to raise funds to buy the captive Jews back. The campaign succeeded beyond everyone's expectations, and while Maimonides was not yet famous, it established his reputation as a community leader who cared for his people. According to a marriage document found in Fustat, which he signed, he already held the honorary title of Rabbi. Some people started referring to him as *ha-Rav ha-Gadol*, or The Great Rabbi. The Islamic authorities began to call him, unofficially, *Ra'is al-Yahud*, or Head of the Jews. Other rabbis already consulted him regularly about legal matters, mostly from other Egyptian towns. Only later would a general stream of questions come from other countries as well.

Maimonides felt he could serve the community in many ways. One of his earliest efforts was to unify and integrate the ritual practices; the split, a symptom of the rift between the two groups of the Jewish community—the Babylonians and the Palestinians.

The Babylonians divided the readings of the Torah's text so that the cycle took a year. The Palestinians initiated a cycle of three years. They did not share many of their rituals, attended separate synagogues and while they celebrated the same holidays, they did not do so in the exact same manner. Maimonides examined the reasons and decided that there was no basis of Law to any of these differences, and therefore found them not only unnecessary, but inappropriate. He did all he could to unify the two groups—but encountered bitter opposition which caused him much trouble.

Another situation he tried to remedy involved the order of prayers. The Babylonian congregation was accustomed to praying in silence, then listening to the cantor repeating the same prayer aloud. Satisfied that their own requirement for prayer had already been accomplished by the silent prayer, people stood around chatting and did not pay any attention to the cantor's prayer. Maimonides felt this was an offense against God, and tried to have the cantor recitation put first, with the silent prayer accompanying it. The congregations did not particularly object to the arrangement—but the new nagid did.

Perhaps he was not exactly new. Yahua Zuta, the old plotter, had succeeded in returning to power by bribing Saladin. No love existed between Zuta and Maimonides, who openly challenged Zuta's authority, and seriously endangered himself by doing so. Zuta was perfectly capable of presenting Maimonides' behavior to Saladin as treason, a crime punishable by death. A little later, that was exactly what he did, but for the moment he bided his time.

In 1172 Maimonides wrote one of his most important letters, the Epistle to Yemen. The Shiite Muslims cruelly persecuted the Yemenite Jews. At the same time, a renegade Jew who had recently converted to Islam tried to persuade the Jews that Islam replaced Judaism as the true religion. As the troubles escalated, a stranger appeared in Yemen, who proclaimed himself to be the forerunner of the Messiah. He performed miracles, commanded the Jews to divide their money among the poor and altogether created a mood of hysteria. Many succumbed to the pressure. Some converted to Islam, while others followed the messianic pretender. The leader of the Jewish community, Jacob Alfayumi, decided to approach Maimonides for advice on the matter.

Maimonides understood the situation very well, having witnessed similar occurrences in Spain and in Fez. Despite his anger and sorrow, the Epistle to Yemen is a calm, loving letter. It does not convey the thundering anger dominating the Epistle on Apostasy which he wrote in Fez. He reviews why throughout history, the Jews have been persecuted though never conquered, and why the special animosity which Christians and Muslims feel toward Judaism exists. He encouraged the Yemenite Jews to stick to their faith and know that deliverance will come. Against his better judgement, since he disliked putting a date on divine revelations, Maimonides even related an old tradition he had received from his father, and his grandfather before him, down to the generation of the destruction of the Temple. This tradition revealed the date when the spirit of prophecy would dwell again among the Jews, a necessary forerunner to the Coming of the Messiah. The date, 1216, was far enough in the future to prove that the messianic pretender was an impostor, and near enough to encourage and give hope.

Next, he carefully proved the falseness and inadequacy of the renegade who tried to convince the Jews that Islam had replaced Judaism as the true religion. He followed the renegade's arguments, showed how they had been tried and proven wrong before and how they were connected to the stupidity of astrology and magic. He further discussed the nature of prophecy, and advised the Jews to keep away from astrology and divination, a chronic cause of much trouble to the Jews, perhaps even the cause of the destruction of the Temple.

Finally, he suggested that the messianic pretender was mentally ill, and fit only for imprisonment. Many other false or self-proclaimed Messiahs tried to confuse the Jews before in other places. He advised the congregation to be careful and continue to believe in their religion, and leave the pretender to his fate. The poor man would probably be seized by the authorities, like so many messianic imposters before him.

The epistle provided relief and comfort to the suffering Yemenite Jews. They followed Maimonides' advice and waited. In the meantime, Maimonides' prediction regarding the self-proclaimed Messiah was correct. The authorities arrested him after about a year of activity. When he was brought in chains to the Muslim ruler, the pretender insisted he was the messenger of God. The ruler, reasonably enough, asked him for some proof. The poor madman, totally convinced of his own divinity, told the ruler that if he cut off his head, he would miraculously be returned to life and his head would reattach itself to his shoulders. The ruler, accepting the challenge, commanded a slave to decapitate the man, and the sad story ended there with just a few strugglers believing that the self-proclaimed Messiah would rise, eventually, from his grave.

In 1174, Saladin's brother Turan Shah conquered Yemen and released the Jews from their troubles. At that time, Maimonides had already developed a very good relationship with the royal family, and therefore Turan Shah treated the Yemenite Jews with particular consideration.

The Yemenite Jews returned Maimonides' affection with respect and admiration bordering on worship, to the point of inserting a special prayer in his honor into their daily ritual. They knew that without the his help, it was entirely possible that the Jews of Yemen would have been absorbed into the Muslim population, disappearing forever. Losing this vital congregation, which is now flourishing in Israel, would have been an immeasurable tragedy for the Jewish world then and now.

# 10

## The Year of Darkness

*Let that day be darkness; let not God regard it from above,*
*neither let the light shine upon it.*

*—Job 2:4*

IN 1174, DAVID PREPARED for a particularly important trip to India, a venture that promised to bring great profits. He invested most of the business' capital in the venture, and various merchants in Fustat trusted him with money and merchandise of their own. As before all of David's trips, Maimonides was extremely anxious, as can be seen from a letter he wrote to David almost at the last moment, probably sending it to the port where David had already boarded the ship. The original is lost; only a copy of the letter exists in someone else's handwriting, but Maimonides' voice comes through loud and clear.

> In the name of the Merciful
> May the Lord strengthen your loins and guard your foot from the trap
> Peace be with the far and the near, said the Lord
> Long will you live, and peace be with you and with your home
> The Lord alone knows the anguish and dreariness in my heart
> When parting from my beloved brother and friend
> May the Lord guard him from harm, and reunite me with

him in Egypt, if the Lord so wills
I wish to let you know I am well,
        Maimonides son of Maimon, blessed is his memory.[1]

Written in the manner of a poem, this letter committed David to the pity and care of the Lord. It told David that Maimonides was well, but only the Lord could know how worried and sorrowful he felt about the parting from his brother and friend. It ended with a little prayer to meet safely again. The usual tense waiting followed, but not for long; bad news arrived quickly. David's boat capsized in the Indian Ocean, killing everyone on board. In one horrible moment, Maimonides' world collapsed.

Since childhood, Maimonides faced trouble and tragedy. He had survived the blows of exile, the death of his stepmother, extreme poverty, the brutal murder of his friend Rabbi Judah ibn Shoshan, the death of his beloved father and recurring danger to his own life. He accepted misfortune every time, and bravely went on with his life. But he could not bear his brother's death. His grief and shock were so immense that they brought on a heart disease, followed by high fever and a serious skin condition due to nervous exhaustion and a deep depression. He was restricted to his bed for an entire year. A while later, he finally started his slow recovery from the intense mourning, but the heart problems and the bouts of depression remained with Maimonides for the rest of his life.

Later, he would write much about the medical side of grief, its treatment, the way in which to try to achieve comfort and regulate one's mind. The description he once gave of a man stricken by sudden mourning echoed the memory of his own trauma. He vividly described a man with a powerful frame, strong voice and a radiant complexion who suddenly heard the horrible news of the death of a loved one: one could see his face turning pale and losing its glow, the sudden hunching of the body, the inability to speak normally. He described how the strength turned into feebleness, the pulse slowed down, the eyes sank in

Typical Coptic-style window at St. Barbaras church, situated
next to Ben Ezra Synagogue in Cairo.
(Photo by Mary Knight)

the sockets. The only reaction from the man would be weeping and arousing the grief further until the body could no longer bear the suffering of the soul. This description is very likely what happened to the strong frame and steady mind Maimonides possessed up until the day of his brother's tragedy.

In addition to the trauma and intolerable pain of the loss of his brother, death was treated in Egypt as a thoroughly communal affair. The public nature of the proceedings put a tremendous strain on Maimonides' shattered nerves. A death in the community was everyone's business. The congregation saw each loss—particularly when caused by unnatural circumstances and to a good man or woman—as a punishment for the community's sins, and they accepted it as a communal bereavement. Before death, if a person was thought fatally ill, the community offered prayers together at the synagogue, fasted together and everyone who could afford it gave alms. After death, much effort was put into organized wailing, and the entire community took a day off work to attend the funeral. They flooded the house of the deceased, offering comfort. If need be, the community assisted in the expenses; everyone discussed wills cheerfully and publicly.

The very day a person died, appointed officials representing the community came to seal the possessions the person left. This custom was based on the talmudic law that defended the rights of orphans and widows. Often, the officials recorded each step in a written document. These officials included a judge, two social services officers, two experts in clothing, jewelry or furnishings, as needed, one person living in the same house, a compatriot of the deceased if he happened to be a foreigner, beadles from the synagogue, a grave digger to measure the corpse and "washers" to take care of the body. Provisions to make a good shroud (needed during the resurrection, which most people firmly believed in), were made.

One can only imagine how Maimonides must have felt during such invasive proceedings. On one hand, no one could love his fellow men more than Maimonides did. On the other hand, no one could have been a more private man. The magnificent set of contradictions that represented the mind and soul of Moses Maimonides usually found a way to reconcile itself with the world around him under whatever circumstances. But under this one tremendous blow, it could not.

The officials found little property to seal, since the gemstones, their most valuable possessions, rested at the bottom of the Indian Ocean. David and Maimonides were full partners, so Maimonides was not unduly persecuted by having furniture and household textiles sealed. He allowed official matters to take their course, respecting the needs of the community. Once it was all over, he took to his bed.

THEORETICALLY, MAIMONIDES was opposed to allowing grief, or any other strong emotion, to influence one's thought process and behavior. He felt that the gift of prophecy disappeared during the time of mourning: the alertness of one's soul and active intellect were reduced, and virtue required a middle between extremes. In his earlier writings, he even states that a wise man could postpone either great joy or great sorrow, and delay the emotional reaction until he ascertained the true consequences of the event. This statement represents theory. In reality, he was unable to realize anything close to his own theories on grief and emotions. He stayed in bed, unable to write or deal with his community work or even worry about the family responsibilities he had to assume as the sole head of a household that included his brother's widow and young daughter. He could cope with none of this. Occasionally he turned to his studies for consolation, but without much success.

This was probably the time he completed the traditional requirement that Jews were instructed to accomplish, but few found the time—copying the entire Torah for themselves, as their own personal copy. Sitting quietly and copying the familiar words of the Torah page by page, could create a comforting occupation to a grieving, tired mind. We do know that at some time during his life, Maimonides did create a copy for himself. It is very unlikely he would have found the time either before or after this period.

In a letter he wrote eight years later to Rabbi Jaffet ben Eliyahu of Acre, Maimonides told his old friend that the passing of time did not help him very much. He could not see a book that belonged to David, or a piece of paper with his handwriting on, without feeling his heart turn inside him and his grief take control again. The letter poignantly expresses the depth of his anguish and continued sense of loss:

Eight years have since passed, and still I mourn, for there is no consolation. What can console me? He grew up on my knees; he was my brother, my pupil. He was engaged in business and earned money that I might stay at home and continue my studies. . . . My one joy was to see him. Now my joy has been changed to darkness; he has gone to eternal home, and left me prostrated in a strange land. Whenever I come across his handwriting or one of his books, my heart grows faint within me, and my grief awakens. In short: "I will go down in the grave unto my son mourning."

He ends the letter saying that if not for the delight in his study of the Torah, and had he not the study of wisdom to divert him from his grief, "I should have succumbed in my affliction."

After a year, Maimonides began to recover, at least physically. His strong constitution and powerful physical frame helped him get over the feverish infections, the handsome face recovered its serene look and the skin disease disappeared. The large dark eyes were no longer sunken in their sockets, as Maimonides regained some of the weight he had lost. He was not entirely well—the depression was too deep-seated and the heart condition remained—and both would trouble him on and off for the rest of his life. After a year of inactivity and withdrawal from daily life there was much to do and he was ready to resume his responsibilities. The family had no money left and no income. Almost all had been lost with his brother in the Indian Ocean, and the little that was left was used during the year of mourning.

Quite a few people lived in the household—his brother's wife and daughter, the wife's sister, Maimonides' sister, a freed slave, a few servants—and they all depended on Maimonides.

The gemstone business was finished; Maimonides knew a lot about trading gems from discussions with his brother, but he had no capital, no merchandise and no desire to engage in trade or to travel. Besides, it would daily remind him of David, and he simply could not tolerate such continuous reminders and pain. He could easily obtain a rabbinical position, but his views on the subject had not changed, and he still did not want to use the Torah for his livelihood. His knowledge and areas of expertise, however, were not limited to religious subjects. Maimonides was extremely well educated in the sciences, in philosophy and in medicine. Practicing any of these arts presented no ethical problems.

After much deliberation, Maimonides decided to practice medicine. Ever since childhood, secretly pursuing Rabbi Maimon's medical books, Maimonides had devoted much time and effort to studying medicine and related subjects simply for pleasure. Now he could put his medical knowledge to good use, helping people and earning a livelihood as well. It was a reasonably well-paying profession, as soon as a doctor acquired a large enough base of patients and until such time, Maimonides knew he could supplement his income by lecturing on philosophy. In his spare time, he would work on his current project, the *Mishneh Torah*. Thinking his plan over, he understood such a lifestyle would force him to be extremely busy, that his depression would be numbed and eventually could even be conquered. Keeping his mind constantly occupied would be the only way to bear a world that could no longer be shared with his beloved brother and friend.

*Above:* View of minaret of the Mosque of al-Aqmar (The Moonlit Mosque) in Cairo. Minarets are a lofty, often slender tower attached to a mosque, having one or more balconies from which the muezzin calls the people to prayer. *Below:* Suspended lamp in inside courtyard of the mosque.
(Photos by Mary Knight)

# 11

# Metamorphosis

When a man assumes a public trust,
he should consider himself as public property.

—*Thomas Jefferson*

THE PLAN WORKED WELL. Maimonides found himself occupied every minute of the day. After a year of seeing little of Maimonides because of his extended physical and mental suffering, the community expressed readiness to accept him in any role. Maimonides entertained no doubt that he would earn his living and provide comfortably for his family.

The metamorphosis from a semi-secluded scholar into a man of affairs required a complete transformation. Not only of mental attitude, but of his total lifestyle, down to the simple matter of what clothes Maimonides chose to wear. Some scholars claim the change even influenced the style of his writing. A cycle of legends that tell about the ease with which it took Maimonides to become court physician, is particularly ironic when viewed in the light of the tremendous effort it actually took. The cycle is entirely mythical, but a few core details in it are fascinating.

One legend has Maimonides coming to Egypt, wearing a white robe and a white turban. A group of dignified Muslims approach the stranger and ask, "What is the name of our lord?" Politely but tersely, Maimonides answers, "Muhammad," and leaves the scene.

Another day the same Muslims see him leaving a synagogue, followed by a group of Jews. Surprised, they say to him, "We thought you are a Muslim. And your name is Muhammad?" Maimonides did not answer immediately, and the crowd became angry; impersonating a Muslim merited death. They dragged Maimonides before the caliph.

The caliph asked him for his true identity, and Maimonides answered "I am a Jew, and the son of a Jew."

"So why are they saying that you pretended to be a Muslim, and that your name was Muhammad?"

"When I came here, people asked me 'What is the name of our lord?' I know that your lord's name is Muhammad. I assumed that if they wanted to know my own name, they would have asked, 'What is your name?" said Maimonides.

The king was impressed and continued the conversation. After some discussion, when he finds out that Maimonides is a doctor, he immediately makes him into chief physician to the court, because of his wisdom.

Of course it took more than a verbal trick to become the court physician, and Maimonides formed his connection with the court not by the aid of an angry crowd, but by a dignified referral. The detail about the white clothes, however, is based on fact. The Fustat population dressed in bright colors, but doctors always wore white, so when Maimonides became a physician, he had to change his style of dress. A Geniza document, ordered and signed by Maimonides in his legal capacity, itemizes the estate of a Jewish physician. Among other matters, the document describes the physician's clothes. The outer garments consisted of a white Turban, a white scarf, a white cloak and a white broad shawl, or tallith, equipped with the ritual tassels. Physical attire was a significant aspect of aesthetic life and social standing and a physician's reputation required the appropriate appearance. Undoubtedly Maimonides dressed himself accordingly.

He chose his new profession wisely. Physicians enjoyed tremendous respect, a high social role and often provided spiritual leadership as well as physical care. They acquired the best secular education, and viewed themselves as disciples of the legendary ancient Greeks. Physicians who achieved positions of distinction were always members of a court. They distanced themselves from politics, and therefore enjoyed all the benefits of the court without any connection to negative aspects such as oppression or war. Physicians saw themselves as a group apart, members of a brotherhood gathered from all religions and countries who could maintain objectivity in all mundane matters. A large number of the doctors of Egypt were minority members, either Christian or Jewish.

Rulers typically collected large numbers of doctors around them: they represented knowledge of books, particularly the ancient science books, and society at this time had a deep respect for books and knowledge. The doctors added distinction to the court. The lower classes also greatly respected knowledge, and even a beginning doctor could rely on a large number of patients consulting him for even the simplest disorder, in large as well as in small towns.

A doctor was invariably extremely busy in his dual role. In a letter addressed to Maimonides later in his career, a student asks some scholarly questions about his new book—*The Guide of the Perplexed*. As the letter continues, the student tells Maimonides about his diet problems. In his reply, Maimonides obligingly answers the philosophical questions—then advises the student about his diet, while complaining to the student about his own bad health at the moment. In another letter, an on-going correspondence with a community official, Maimonides gave the administrative instructions the official required, and then advised the man to discontinue the hire of a cow, because since he would need only one glass of milk in the morning and one at night, he could easily purchase the milk without bothering to take care of the cow. (The man apparently had recovered from an earlier illness after following Maimonides' advice to hire the cow and follow a diet of fresh milk.)

Many distinguished physicians were descendants of families who held their positions for generations. The son inherited a position as court physician from the father. Maimonides did not have such an advantage; he would have to make his own way. Later, though, his son Abraham would inherit Maimonides' position.

Medical lectures were rarely offered, and only in a few places. A medical student apprenticed with an older physician, often with a few physicians in succession. From his mentors, the student learned how to perform practical medicine; he studied medical theory from scientific and medical books, memorizing a tremendous amount of material. The large curriculum intimidated many aspirants. A student had to study the works of Galen and Hippocrates in the original Greek, if possible, and if not, in the complete translations. Summaries and compendiums, prepared in Alexandria in pre-Islamic times, were considered good study aids but not sufficient in themselves. The student read the pre-Islamic and Islamic commentaries on Galen and Hippocrates, though, and also studied the Islamic physician Al-Razi, who died in A.D. 925

After completing his apprenticeship, a young doctor worked in one of the *Bimaristans*, a Persian word meaning "places for the sick." The concept of hospitals came from Iran, where it was developed by Greek-trained physicians. Obtaining the hospital position involved certain difficulties. A student needed letters of recommendation and a *tazkiya*, a certificate of good conduct from the police. Obtaining the tazkiya depended on giving gifts to officials and utilizing good connections. It seems from the literature that only distinguished doctors held permanent positions in the hospitals. Abraham Maimonides held such a position later, as well as inheriting the court-physician position from his father.

The hospitals functioned as charitable institutions. The Fatimids did not have much interest in them, as far as we know, but the Ayyubids generously endowed hospitals. The institutions were amazingly modern in their division into wards, where different diseases and conditions were treated separately— fevers, surgery, eye diseases, etc. A letter in the Geniza was directed to "The Head of the Dysentery Ward, Ramle Hospital, Palestine." Few Jews went to the hospitals, though, because they could not keep the dietary laws there. They preferred to be treated at home, or at the synagogue. Sometimes a physician operated a small private hospital at his home. Other small private hospitals were operated by non-physicians. Some information exists about a wealthy and charitable woman, the wife of a Jewish judge, who operated a hospital from her home, entirely as her own enterprise.

A doctor might work from a store, sometimes sharing it with another doctor or a pharmacist, or from his own house. Patients usually bought medicines at a separate pharmacist's store, but a doctor sometimes mixed complex prescriptions himself on the spot. Such prescriptions usually included twenty or more ingredients, and required minute knowledge of medicinal plants. The list of medicinal plants doctors used comprised three thousand items, out of which a hundred and twenty were considered common.

A doctor's day started at dawn. Often, he ordered his patient to take a special prescription at precisely that time, and wanted to be present during treatment. The doctor visited certain patients every day, and occasionally a patient in another town. Occasionally a doctor would prescribe treatment based on a description of the symptoms, without ever seeing the patient.

Some physicians were poor, but generally the profession paid very well. No one objected to physicians engaging in other businesses as well as medicine and it became a common habit. One of their most popular side business was the book trade. Through their long study period many developed a great love of books and accumulated extensive libraries. Their love of letters also expressed itself through poetry. Some doctors were poets of great renown—such as Judah Halevi, who practiced medicine until he left Spain, and possibly even after his move.

TWO FACTORS MADE MAIMONIDES' transition into this lifestyle a little easier. A physician in those days did not need licensing from a university, or an association, but received his acknowledgment from a prominent, government-authorized physician. Maimonides found such a sponsor easily. The whole community knew that he was already well trained in medicine and Maimonides was in high demand for his philosophical lectures, which very nicely tided him through the rough spots.

In addition to developing his medical practice, Maimonides kept up with his writing, and continued to discharge communal duties, as evidenced from a few documents that show that he functioned very actively as a rabbi during this time. If all that was not enough to keep him occupied, new clashes with the nagid, Zuta soon began.

Zuta's enmity was extremely dangerous, but Maimonides ignored the risk and openly joined the opposition. The nagid regarded Maimonides as an upstart and a foreigner, and was furious with his interference. During one of Saladin's campaigns against the Christians in Palestine, Zuta's son, who assisted his father regularly, found three immigrant Jews and brought charges against them to the governor, claiming that they were conspiring against Saladin. The governor, who saw no reason to doubt the nagid's son's word, had them severely beaten and thrown in jail.

As often happens during times of war, strong prejudices against foreigners began to brew even without Zuta's help. Maimonides, who came to Egypt from Palestine, the land of the Christian enemies, was a natural suspect of espionage. Zuta denounced him as a foreigner involved in subversive activities and claimed that since Saladin appointed him the nagid, Maimonides' opposition exposed him as a traitor.

In the meantime, two of the Jews previously arrested died in jail, and the entire community felt threatened. Friends advised Maimonides to hide out for a while, away from Zuta's attention. Many legends claim he hid in a secluded cave, and in this case, such legendary claims are verified by a traveler from Toledo who wished to meet Maimonides. Apparently, the traveler came to Egypt after a journey that took nine months, arriving to find that Maimonides had disappeared. No one wished to tell him where

Maimonides was hiding, but the traveler refused to give up his search and two weeks later finally found him in the cave. Maimonides was delighted to see a countryman from his beloved Spain. The traveler later wrote that Maimonides accepted his situation calmly, and spent his time in the cave working on his book, the *Mishneh Torah*. Maimonides likely enjoyed the temporary peace and quiet of the cave, and the luxury of so much free time to devote to writing.

He could not stay there forever, and fortunately, political change was about to occur. When Saladin took the office of viceroy, he had to consider his relationship with Nureddin of Syria. Even though they were on friendly terms, Nurredin certainly was not going to let him become independent, which was exactly what Saladin wanted. Nurredin planned to take charge of Egypt himself, and control of the entire area surrounding the kingdom of Jerusalem, thinking this would enable him to eventually wipe out the Christians. But Saladin's luck held and in 1174, before accomplishing his plans, Nurredin suddenly died and left a young child as his legal heir. A regent, the emir of Allepo, ruled the country in the child's name. Total chaos ensued in the subordinate states—and one by one they declared independence of Damascus.

King Amalric of Jerusalem saw this as his chance and planned to attack Syria, annex it to Jerusalem and then move on to attack Egypt. The plan would have undoubtedly succeeded, but then a strange thing happened. As a mirror image to the events in Syria with Nurredin, Amalric suddenly died, leaving an heir who was not only a child, but stricken with leprosy, or Hansen Disease. The kingdom of Jerusalem also came under the rule of a regent.

The emir of Allepo, guardian to the young king of Damascus, prepared for the civil war that was about to break in Syria. He approached Saladin for help, and Saladin, marching with his army, subdued the rebelling states, and returned them to the dominion of the young king. In 1175, however, the fickle emir of Allepo changed his alliances, bonded with the emir of Mosul, and attacked Saladin. Tired of the petty strife, Saladin nonetheless realized this act had created the opportunity he needed. With his usual ease he succeeded the attack, and declared himself the king of both Egypt and Syria.

In 1176, Saladin returned to Egypt from his latest campaign, planning to move his official capital from Damascus to Cairo. The opposition to Zuta, to which Maimonides still belonged, decided to use this opportunity to finally get rid of the usurper, once and for all.

IN DAMASCUS, THE HEAD of the Jewish community, referred to as the "exilarch," was always occupied by a direct descendent of the house of King David. The Jewish community felt that since Cairo was to become the new capital, the exilarch should reside there, and govern the Jews in both countries. Saladin responded favorably to the suggestion, and invited the exilarch, Judah ben Josiah, to accompany him to Cairo.

Judah ben Josiah, a descendent of a long line of exilarchs, met Maimonides and recognized in him a great scholar, a member of the opposition to Zuta and a distant relative—a descendent of the House of David like himself. He asked Maimonides to assist him in legal matters, and even issued an ordinance that made Maimonides' decisions final and not subject to challenge. This association pushed Maimonides further on the path to spiritual leadership of the Jews.

Maimonides' financial situation began to greatly improve as well. True, he did not receive payment for working with the exilarch on communal matters; however, his medical career was developing well and there was less need to lecture as much as before, which pleased him as he continued to dislike this activity. The *Mishneh Torah* benefited from the extra time he now had to devote to his writing. His health improved, and the exciting events kept his depression at bay. As time passed, Maimonides became more and more influential in Jewish affairs and his reputation as a legal expert spread over most of the Jewish world, with the responsa increasingly occupying his time. Answering questions regarding the Law remained one of his favorite forms of writing and teaching throughout his entire life, even when he was no longer writing full-length books.

In 1176 Maimonides had the opportunity to issue the edicts against Jews who followed the Karaite traditions. He started by pronouncing the judgement that women who followed the Karaite rituals of purifications, instead of the rabbinical ones, should be divorced and lose their dowry. This edict changed life within the home—the core of the Jewish community—and became permanent. It accomplished what Maimonides wanted, because the decision appealed to the women's practical nature. Unlike the men, women had little interest in the theory of religion. Most married women preferred changing the purification right, not a very difficult affair, to going through an unpleasant divorce and losing some money in the bargain.

With everything that has been written about Maimonides and the Karaites, it is easy to assume he waged a full-fledged war against them. In actuality, he had no intention of fighting them at all and most of his judgements were meant to entice the Karaites to rejoin rabbinic Judaism. None of the edicts were intended to humiliate or alienate them. Probably due to his tolerance, he was able to win many over. The Karaites have become extinct in the Arab world, and some scholars believe they all converted to Islam. The evidence shows that many did not do that, and instead a large number of them returned to rabbinic Judaism.

Regaining the Karaite community was a victory for Maimonides. The ability to maintain tolerance toward other traditions as well as religions, despite his deep commitment to his own, was one of Maimonides' most influential characteristics. The twelfth century was not a tolerant time, and the coincidence of having Saladin, famous for the same quality, functioning at the same time and the same place, is remarkable in history.

The Convent of St. George in Old Cairo, built between 1021–1094. It connects by typical medieval gates and stairs to the Coptic compound of the Old Cairo area, and contains decorations from the Fatimid period. (Photo by Mary Knight)

# 12

## The *Mishneh Torah*

On these grounds, I, Moses the son of Maimon the Sefardi, bestirred myself,
and, relying on the help of God, blessed be He, intently studied all these
works, with the view of putting together the results obtained from them in
regard to what is forbidden or permitted, clean or unclean, and the other rules
of the Torah—all in plain language and terse style, so that thus the entire Oral
Law might become systematically known to all.

—*Moses Maimonides*

IN 1180, WHEN HE WAS about forty-five years old, Maimonides
finished his monumental code, the *Mishneh Torah*.[1] He worked
on this book for ten years, on and off, though not in sequence.
He completed various sections in different times. Maimonides
understood that this was his greatest work to date, perhaps the
most important he would ever write. The scope of the book is so
immense, it is almost inconceivable to realize that it was composed by a single man. A work of this magnitude is much more
likely to be written by many people through several generations,
with an editor, or a group of editors, creating the final version.

Before starting to write the book in 1170, Maimonides completed a preliminary work called *Sefer ha-Mitzvot* (Book of
Commandments). The book stands on its own, but it also serves
as a proper introduction to the *Mishneh Torah*. Unlike the *Mishneh Torah*, which is written in Hebrew, he wrote the *Sefer ha-
Mitzvot* in Arabic.

According to talmudic tradition, God gave the biblical Moses
613 divine commandments[2] at Mount Sinai. Many more exist, and
no general agreement exists about, or final decision ever decreed
which commandments deserved to be included in the divine list, or
enumeration, and which were to be excluded. Maimonides needed

an exact list to work with when writing the *Mishneh Torah*, and decided to create a final and undisputed version.

In the introduction to *Sefer ha-Mitzvot*, Maimonides states plainly that he wrote the book as a preliminary to the *Mishneh Torah*. He explains that he had no intention of delving into details, and only wished to enumerate the commands. He separated them into two groups. The 248 positive commandments[3] correspond to the number of limbs in the human body. Each limb invites a person to "Perform a commandment with me." The 365 negative commandments[4] correspond to the days of the solar year, as if to say, "Do not transgress this day." The book explains in detail how the commandments are counted, based on a system of fourteen principles. Maimonides' new classification was innovative and objective in its approach, and deviated from the systems of his predecessors. After the book was completed, he would approach the task of the writing the *Mishneh Torah* with confidence.

The *Mishneh Torah* is a summary of the entire body of Jewish law—not only Law for the years of the Diaspora—but for a free State of Israel. It includes laws that no other person would have considered at that time, because they could not be observed following the destruction of the Temple, and without a free state. Maimonides expected the State of Israel to come into being much sooner than history permitted. He believed the event would take place shortly after 1216, only 36 years after the book reached the public. Undoubtedly he would have been somewhat distressed to learn that the Jews would have to wait another 768 years until the State of Israel would be created in 1948, but it is unlikely that he would have been permanently discouraged.

> As it is impossible for God to cease to exist, so is Israel's destruction and disappearance from the world unthinkable.

His code was timeless, and would serve just as well in the twenty first century as in the thirteenth.

The book functions as a complete legal system, written in the format of a code, and it forever changed the entire landscape of rabbinic literature. It gives the final decision of each law, without discussion or explanation of how these decisions were reached. Before the existence of the *Mishneh Torah*, a person attempting to study the Oral Law had to grasp the Talmud, which is an intensely complicated work. But with the *Mishneh Torah*, if a person is well versed in the Torah, he or she can understand the Oral Law without the necessity of referring to additional sources. Despite many accusations to the contrary, Maimonides never intended it to supplant the Talmud. He greatly encouraged the readers to continue with their studies and to delve deeply into the Talmud, but the *Mishneh Torah* can introduce a person to a life-long learning experience with ease and comfort.

The book is written in an elegant Hebrew style. Not the biblical Hebrew—which would have caused some limitations, and not talmudic Aramaic, which was too difficult—but in the versatile Hebrew of the Mishna. The book is unique in that the language is concise, and the prose vigorous and easy to understand and it was written for the broadest possible audience.

The *Mishna Torah* completely reorganizes the laws in a clear and logical system. Maimonides created an order and structure based on a new topical-pedagogical arrangement which did not follow the sequence of the Mishnah or the Talmud and was an ambitious attempt at classification that had not been seen before. Its fascination also lies in its synthesis of many cultures; it fuses Jewish law and Aristotelian philosophy, and draws on French, Greek and Spanish authorities, though they are not named. The book is divided into fourteen groups, each constituting a book. They are further divided into sections, chapters and paragraphs.[5]

Scholars often speculated on Maimonides' reasons for creating the *Mishneh Torah*. The questions they raised were never resolved, neither during his life nor through the eight centuries since his death. The first and foremost accusation is the claim that Maimonides intended it to supplant the Talmud. This is based on one of his own statements. Maimonides stated that anyone who is familiar with the Torah can read the *Mishneh Torah* and acquire complete understanding of the Oral Law without opening another book. In addition, he never mentioned the names of the scholars of the Talmud—the Tannaim and the Amoraim. Some detractors went further by saying that Maimonides had pronounced that all other books could be destroyed or burned—an accusation Maimonides not only flatly denied, but by which he was amused by its stupidity.

In fact, Maimonides said, that a person who knows the Torah can also understand the Oral Law after reading the *Mishneh Torah*—nothing else is needed. But Maimonides only meant the book as an overview, a beginning of the road to scholarship. Two very important letters show his attitude toward the subject. In letters written at different times to Rabbi Pinchas ben Meshulam, the dayyan of Alexandria, and to Rabbi Jonathan Cohen of Lunel, he reminded them that he states in the introduction of the *Mishneh Torah* that he wrote it to ease the student's first exposure to the Oral Law. The Talmud is tremendously complicated, full of arguments, commentaries and contradictory statements. It invariably confuses and discourages the beginner. The *Mishneh Torah* smooths the bumps, and when one finished studying it, as a matter of course he would turn to the Talmud. In many passages of his book, Maimonides mentions the Talmud again and again.

In this respect, the *Mishneh Torah* is much like the Mishna, whose author, Rabbi Judah ha-Nasi, did not confuse the issue with interpretation either, and certainly did not mention all the sages he was indebted to, only a selected number. Maimonides lists many of these names in the introduction to the *Mishneh Torah*, so it cannot be said that he ignored them. In his introduction to the *Mishneh Torah* in *A Maimonides Reader*, Twerski says that:

> Although confident about the need, value, and ultimate acceptance of his code, Maimonides anticipated criticism and opposition on the grounds of his a) having omitted source references and presented unilateral, unsubstantiated decisions and b) having included a heady dose of philosophic exposition and comment. He also felt that jealous people "would defame its praiseworthy features and pretend" that

such a summary was totally superfluous for them. Such criticism was indeed forthcoming and it markedly influenced the spread and study of the *Mishneh Torah*.

In an interesting and self-revealing letter to his student, Joseph ibn Aknin, Maimonides wrote that originally he meant to write the book entirely for his own use. The concise writing would work as a digest, to help him find specific matters if his memory failed him in his old age. As the writing advanced, he realized that the book could become not only a digest, but a code for the entire body of Jewish scholars.

To understand Maimonides' approach to the *Mishneh Torah*, two concepts should be clear: his messianic views, and his life-long relationship with the biblical Moses. Maimonides was convinced that the year 1216 would bring the return of prophesy. This secret date had been handed down for generations in his family and the event was meant to precede the Coming of the Messiah. The socio-politic, religious and cultural turbulence in the world—which seemed to match the descriptions of the last days before the Coming—also convinced Maimonides that the Messiah would arrive very soon.

In the light of Maimonides' rationalism and dislike of Kabbalistic tradition and mystical thought, his messianic preoccupations and claims may seem strange, but his views on the nature of the Messiah explain them. It must be remembered that Maimonides did not conceive of the Messiah as a supernatural being. He expected a king—even a relative—since the Messiah had to be a descendent of the House of David. Naturally then, he would be a mortal man (though long lived), unusually wise and well versed in prophecy. He expected that the king/Messiah would wage war, conquer Palestine, and—just like the biblical Moses—would once again lead the Jews to the Promised Land. In the new free State of Israel, the Jews would live normal lives, though long and healthy—and most important—would be permitted to study the Torah and follow their own laws.

The *Mishneh Torah*, therefore, was meant to serve as the

Israeli Constitution. In it, Maimonides made available all the laws that existed—from those given on Mount Sinai up to his own time—for the new nation in its homeland. He saw no need to credit sources or present arguments. Principles and laws were all that were required. In his mind's eye, he saw the *Mishneh Torah* following the Torah, not the Mishna.

The name and divisions of his book support this view. In Hebrew, the second title for the *Mishneh Torah* is *Yad ha-Hazaka*, or *The Mighty Hand*, based on the last verse of the Pentateuch: "And in all that mighty hand, and in all the great terror which Moses shewed in the sight of all Israel." The numerical value of the word "yad" in Hebrew is fourteen. Maimonides divided the book into fourteen parts, making a special effort to make sure that this was the number, though it is clear that the material could have been more comfortably divided into a different number.

Maimonides was born on Nisan 14, on Passover Eve, and heard the tales of the biblical Moses after whom he was named—since early childhood. Maimonides believed that Moses was the greatest of the prophets. He demonstrates four points that made him believe that the biblical Moses was superior to all others: he received his revelations directly from God, without the intervention of any other entity, such as an angel; he communed with God not in a dream, but in a normal state of consciousness; he did not dissolve or burn, as some other prophets did, but maintained himself whole and he maintained prophetic ability continuously, not in intervals.

Maimonides held that the biblical Moses achieved his state—similar to that of an angel or a pure spirit—because he liberated himself from desire, from the tyranny of his senses and from the power of his imagination. Legends and folklore show, by the way, how much the Jews also accepted the similarity and connection between the two leaders, so much so that the famous saying, circulating even during Maimonides' lifetime, was later inscribed on his grave: "From Moses to Moses there were none like Moses." The similarities between the two men were based on the facts that both started life during a time of persecution;

both lived in Egypt; both had many miracles attributed to them and were strongly involved with the king; both were hounded by enemies all their lives and both were leaders of the Jews.

THE RELATIONSHIP or connection between the biblical Moses and Moses Maimonides, started, according to a variant legend, even before Maimonides was born, and is attributed to the prophetic dream that Rabbi Maimon had before he married Maimonides' mother:

> This event happened to the father of the Rambam, Rabbi Maimon, rest his soul. From his youth Rabbi Maimon contemplated Torah and wisdom, inquiring into wonders and looking at the deepest and exalted secrets of the Torah; and these secrets, their keys were saved for elders, who had already advanced in wisdom. And Rabbi Maimon was so deep into the Torah that he refused to marry, because, he said, "my soul longs for the Torah only." The years passed and he was still unmarried.
>
> One day Maimon lied under a fig tree in his garden, and a tiny bee started walking on his face. He woke up, but immediately fell asleep again. In his dream he saw the five books of Moses' Torah. He started reading, and suddenly saw Moses, son of Amram, giving the Torah. He turned to Rabbi Maimon and said: "The Lord of Heaven and Earth be blessed. He will give you a son who will write *Mishneh Torah*, and light the eyes of all Israel; he will be a holy man, perfect in the quality of spirit and soul, a teacher and a leader of his people."
>
> While our Rabbi Moses was still speaking, Elijah the Prophet appeared and said: Maimon, get up and go to nearby Córdoba, and take as wife the daughter of the butcher there.
>
> When Rabbi Maimon woke up, he traveled to Córdoba and married the butcher's daughter, as Elijah the Prophet said. And the woman gave birth to Moses, the Rambam. The mother did not have the privilege of raising her son Moses: she died in childbirth.[6]

A story that had been recorded after Maimonides finished the *Mishneh Torah*, was based on another dream. It cannot be called a legend, because it is very likely that Maimonides actually had this dream, and either told someone or wrote it down himself. According to this story, when Maimonides finished the book, he understood its value. However, he also expected tremendous objections and was worried about them. He believed some people would object to his having omitted the references to his sources, and knew some may not like his presentation of unsubstantiated opinions. He expected many to object to the inclusion of non-Jewish philosophy. Further, he knew that his enemies would do anything to detract from the book even if they believed it to be good, out of jealousy and ill will.

As the story continues, one night all was done. There was nothing left to correct, nothing to reread, nothing to ponder. In a state of deep anxiety, drained and exhausted, Maimonides went to sleep, and had a profound and significant dream:

> The night after he completed the book *Mishneh Torah*, his father, Rabbi Maimon, came to him in a dream, and with him was our teacher Moses ben Amram. Rabbi Maimon said "My son, this man that you see with me is our teacher, Moses ben Amram." And he added: "My son, we came to see the book you have written." He got up and gave them the book, and they looked at it and said: "May thy strength increase for the book you have written."[7]

One can imagine that even the great rationalist, the man who disdained any supernatural inclination and vigorously criticized mysticism, could not have resisted a sign of approval from the spirits of Rabbi Maimon, his beloved and honored father, and Moses ben Amram, the greatest prophet who had ever lived.

# 13

# Marriage and Family

As concerning marriage, it is certain that this is in harmony with reason,
if the desire for physical union be not engendered solely by bodily beauty,
but also by the desire to beget children and to train them up wisely;
and moreover, if the love of both, to wit, of the man and of the woman,
is not caused by bodily beauty only, but also by freedom of soul.

—*Benedict de Spinoza*

MARRIAGE AND FAMILY REPRESENTED the cornerstone of the Jewish community, an obligation to God. Neither a man nor a woman could aspire to spiritual wholeness without achieving these states. A woman had no choice whether to marry or not—when she reached her early teens, her father arranged for her marriage. This may sound harsh to the modern reader, but at that time such was the matter of course. The time of her engagement promised great fun—choosing clothes, jewelry and household goods, congratulations, celebrations and many joyous preparations. From early childhood, marriage and motherhood were a girl's destiny, her hope and her career. Love-marriages, in the modern sense, and the idea of choosing one's husband, did not exist. A young girl had no close contact with young men, at least theoretically, and did not have faith in her own ability to make such a momentous decision for herself, anyway. She trusted her father implicitly, and a girl and her family could only hope that the husband would turn out to be a good match, and that love would eventually develop within the marriage.

To this end, a father carefully checked a potential groom's character and habits. A father would not marry his daughter to a person he did not like, and would be anxious that the marriage prove a success in their divorce-oriented society. Many surviving letters show that fathers, unquestionably the patriarchal heads of the family, treated their daughters kindly and with great love. Even after an unhappy marriage and divorce, many younger women elected to remarry and often had additional children. Generally, only divorced or widowed older women remained unmarried by choice.

A man generally followed the same path, with two marked differences. First, even an older man almost always chose to remarry. Second, if a man was a recognized scholar, he could declare that the Torah was his true love and that he wished to be permitted to avoid marriage. Such was a controversial decision though. The community chose its leaders from the ranks of scholars; and one could not serve unless he were married. The single-state status barred such a scholar from a political career and confined him strictly to academics, causing a solitary existence in both personal and professional spheres. In this gregarious, sociable society it took great courage to remain single—or a true abhorrence of the married state.

Maimonides' natural inclination leaned toward a solitary, academic existence, and his love of study was boundless. Under different circumstances, he may well have chosen to remain unattached and free to study. In a letter he wrote later in life to his student Joseph ibn Aknin, Maimonides described the Torah as his beloved wife, and the secular sciences as her rival concubines. A humorous description, touched with a subtle sense of fun, it nevertheless contained a measure of truth. Moving into public affairs probably felt a little like betraying his true destiny. In the *Mishneh Torah*, he stated that a man who loved the Torah and continued to study it all his life, could remain unmarried without committing a sin, unless he suffered from sexual desires. Most scholars agree that Maimonides often based his approach to the Law on his personal experience. His own ambivalence regarding this important matter must have caused him much anguish.

When nearing the age of forty, Maimonides finally married.

Muallaqa Church. "The Hanging Church,"called so because it sits above the east tower of the Fortress of Babylon, seeming to hang over it. It is one of the oldest churches in Egypt, serving since the fourth century. (Photo by Mary Knight)

The date is so much debated, that it is useless to try and pinpoint it, but it seems likely that the marriage took place in 1175. Unless someday scholars uncover a cache of previously unknown personal letters, we may never know the mental process that led him to his decision to marry. Perhaps the unrelenting loneliness after his brother David's death finally pushed him in this direction. The pressure to produce an heir to his distinguished family lineage may also have decided it; Maimonides saw himself, after all, as a scion of the House of David. Perhaps he was troubled by sexual desire, though he would have fought valiantly against that. Despite Judaism's positive approach to sex within marriage, Maimonides often quoted Aristotle, saying that the sense of touch is our disgrace. In *The Guide of the Perplexed* he added that people must avoid speaking about anything relating to sexual relations. This was an area of life that was to remain secret. It is also possible that he thought marriage would help him in his medical career; people may have mistrusted an unmarried physician. Perhaps the simple human realization that time was advancing on him decided the matter.

Again, many speculations exist about a first wife from Spain; with some respected scholars assuming that the woman he married in Fustat was his second wife. However, many other scholars disagree, since no substantiating record exists for the first marriage besides a few legends and oral traditions. This lack of information stands in stark contrast to the many records pertaining to the marriage in Fustat.

The silence surrounding the claim of a first family, with the wife and two children dying upon arrival in Egypt or shortly after, is incongruous with what is known about Maimonides' character and penchant for correspondence, and his personal relationships. Particularly in light of his many letters regarding his love for his son Abraham and his sorrow for the death of his little daughter, which are full of strong emotions. Is it possible that he would not mention the alleged horrible tragedy of his supposed first family when writing about that time? It is very suspicious that not a single letter of consolation would remain from his many friends in Spain, Palestine and Fez. When his brother died, Maimonides was bedridden for an entire year, stricken by grief. When he wrote about David, eight years after the tragedy, he was still unable to overcome his anguish. It is not likely that such a sensitive man would not have committed to some record the existence and subsequent loss of his wife and children, especially in view of the other carefully recorded history and progression of his life that we have. We are fortunate to know something about the woman Maimonides married in Fustat, though there is no record of her name. Much of the information we have comes from the historian Alkifeti, a contemporary of Maimonides' son Abraham.

MAIMONIDES' WIFE WAS the daughter of a noble old family that boasted many scholars and international merchants. Her father was Rabbi Mishael Halevi; a letter Maimonides later wrote him shows Rabbi Mishael to be an admirable man. Maimonides wrote to him with utmost respect, even deference. With Maimonides, one had to earn such treatment; rank and age would not have been enough.

His bride brought him many relatives—five brothers, and probably a few sisters. Her brother Uziel, called Abu Almaali by his Arabic-speaking contemporaries, was a writer of some importance. He became a good friend to Maimonides, and later married his sister. Such close relations-marriages were quite common in those days, when family connections were of high value and worth careful planning. Abu Alracha, one of Uziel's and Maimonides' sister's sons, became a physician like his uncle Maimonides, and was considered a clever doctor. The records show that Maimonides personally trained him, and that he later further studied under another physician and also held a distinguished position at one of the hospitals.

While we do not know Maimonides' wife's name, and there are no paintings that could bring her closer to us, much can be deduced from period writing. We know she was a wealthy young woman. She would have been able to afford the elegant clothes so readily available in Fustat, beautifully made from the finest silks and linens and intricately embroidered. She would probably have worn dazzling gold and pearl jewelry, including earrings, necklaces, bracelets, anklets and rings, and because of her wealth, perhaps even precious emeralds, rubies and sapphires. She probably was carefully made up, according to the sophisticated habits of the women at that time and place, and used perfumes lavishly. And her hair and nails may have been professionally done, probably tinted with reddish henna by a personal maid, trained since early childhood to dress society women.

Coming from noble family, which typically stressed their important lineage, would have formed his wife's character. It was customary for women of nobility, even required from women of her class, to give alms and help the sick and poor. She would have socialized extensively with many friends among the young women of Fustat, and involved herself in all the community affairs shared by this group of women. It can be assumed that Maimonides' wife was at the time of her marriage, very young, either in her teens or just out of them, because bearing children represented the most important reason for their marriage. The community at that time considered it necessary to allow a woman as many years as possible to produce healthy children, particularly in light of the heavy child mortality rate of the era.

The scholarly family took education very seriously and members were expected to study the Torah for the rest of their lives. They developed a great love of books, and pursued secular education as well as the religious with great interest. A man's worth was measured by his scholarship and he could not serve as an official without it. Egypt was not the highest in learning— some scholars believe it was the least educated of all Jewish communities—but nevertheless it showed a great love of study. Parents brought up their children to appreciate the value of learning; even the poorest families met the school fees before paying for many other essentials.

Since much of the elementary school education served as preparation for participation in the synagogue service, it was obligatory only for boys. Women, even though they attended the service, did not participate in reading it. Boys had incentives to learn; they were often publicly honored by reading selected texts in the synagogue. Community leaders also encouraged secular learning, and even actively teaching Muslim and Christian boys, for the sake of good relationship with the non-Jewish neighbors. Female education was voluntary and less subject to structure. Many girls simply attended school with their brothers and followed the same curriculum. Others went to girls schools. One of Maimonides' surviving letters discusses a difficult situation with a class of strong-minded little girls who liked their teacher so much, that despite his blindness, and other problems that may have required his leaving that post, they refused to study with anyone but him. Even orphan girls' education was taken care of by charity, private or communal.

Many women developed exstensive knowledge of religious studies, so much so that they were sought after as teachers for boys as well as girls. Some schools were kept by a family—husband and wife, brother and sister. Often the woman ran the entire business. Such knowledge mattered not only for professional business, but for a good marriage as well. Even the Talmud maintains that a rabbi, or any scholarly official, must marry a scholar's daughter, so that she would know how to run his household. There is no doubt that Maimonides' wife's family carefully trained her properly in religious subjects.

In addition to their theoretical studies, girls were trained in crafts. Some women developed expertise in calligraphy, often becoming professional scribes. A beautifully written letter survives in which a female scribe named Miriam[1] added a note of apology for the imperfection of her handwriting: while she was writing, her baby was nursing! Girls also trained in sewing, including embroidery. A girl who could embroider well never lacked employment when she reached the age to start earning a living—a booming embroidery industry existed in Fustat. Wealthier women enjoyed embroidery as a hobby. Maimonides' wife was quite likely an accomplished needlewoman.

We can expect that Maimonides' wife was a most suitable wife for the future nagid, but how she might have felt about their marriage is more difficult to discern. Did Maimonides' bride realize she was about to marry one of the two greatest men of her generation? Probably not. She might have assumed that Saladin would go down in history, but as far as she knew, many members of the Jewish community were at least as important as her new husband. However, we might assume that she accepted her father's choice happily; Maimonides had a lot to offer: he came from an exceptionally good family; he had some fame, a very good income, a bright future and the tremendous respect of the community for his scholarship, not only in Fustat, but in the entire Jewish and Muslim world.

Although considerably older than his bride, Maimonides was an extremely handsome man with a charismatic personality, and despite his ambiguity toward women as a group, was naturally capable of intense love. He never wrote about his love for his wife, an unseemly act by his standards (not to mention the standards of the time), but the way in which he describes his love for other people, such as his father, his brother, his lost little daughter and his son Abraham, shows a rare depth of feeling. By tradition, his inclination would be to honor and cherish a wife. On a personal level, she came into his life when he was lonely and depressed.

Trying to understand Maimonides' attitudes toward sex and especially within his own marriage is a complicated matter. As for his own ethics and lifestyle, he emerges as extremely restrained and regulated. In one revealing sentence in a medical book, he says that "whoever desires the continuance of health should drive his thoughts from coitus all he can."

In the *Mishneh Torah*, Maimonides described his ideal marital relations. In it he explained that though the wife is always permitted, a wise man conducts himself with sanctity, and should not be found with his wife all the time (Maimonides added humorously, "like a rooster"), but only on Friday nights, and only if he feels up to it. He should only have sex in the middle of the night, when the digestion process is in the optimum state, and never after a bath. Sex should not be performed during the day, nor with a lamp at night, to preserve modesty.

A man should not indulge in frivolity, nor should the conversation between man and wife ever be vulgar. Neither of them should be intoxicated, lazy or depressed, and the wife should not be asleep. If the wife is not willing, the man should never coerce her, because sexual intercourse must always be carried out with the consent of both, and while they are both happy. The husband is permitted to converse and jest a little, to put his wife at her ease, and then have sex with modesty and without impudence. The husband and wife must separate immediately after intercourse.

There is more to this effect in his other books, all showing an unusually strict attitude toward sex. Maimonides' attitudes are a little surprising, because Judaism views marital sex as a gift from God. Not only as the means for procreation, which is indeed considered its primary purpose, but also as a means for strengthening the union between husband and wife. Many sages considered it a man's duty, and a woman's right, to have sex every Friday night. A woman could sue for divorce if her husband refused to fulfil this marital obligation.

ONCE MARRIED, MAIMONIDES' wife likely continued to lead the privileged life of a member of the upper classes, though the lives of many contemporary women were not quite so easy. Not so much because of their inequality to men, but because men viewed them as a separate group. The strained communication between males and females occurred mostly because a man was only permitted to associate with his female relatives and the household members. Even letters were subjected to the strictest etiquette.

A man was forbidden to mention his wife's name or to address her directly in correspondence. He wrote to his mother, or another relative, mentioning his wife only in passing. He did not call her "my wife" but only "the one who is with me," or "the children and their mother," or even as "the house," because the word "wife" carried sexual connotation. In a rather amusing letter, an elder brother sent his regrets that he had never met his

"younger brother's house, who had just given birth to a boy."
During the twelfth century, the taboo slowly eroded. Maimonides himself broke it often, but not with ease. In a letter to
a disciple, he wrote: "The Law forbids sending greetings to a
woman; it does not forbid praying for her. Therefore, peace be
upon you and peace be upon your house."

Despite many misconceptions regarding the place of women
in medieval society, the Jewish community did not treat them as
chattel. Theoretically, they were confined to the home sphere.
The biblical saying, "*Kol Kevoda Bat Melech Penima*" (Psalms
45:13) means, literally, that a princess is most honored within
the home. However, note the word "princess." Inside her home,
a woman functioned as the center of the family, the one who lit
the candles and represented the mystical Queen of the Sabbath
and the Shechina, or God's spirit. She was highly respected by
her husband and children, and if the folktales, legends, songs
and oral traditions are to be believed, many marriages were
happy and successful.

Men and women honored the required social separation
more in theory than in practice. Many single women had to support themselves and their children. They participated in the economic life, bought and sold property, went to court, traveled
extensively, trained in various professions and initiated divorce
proceedings. Even married women operated businesses apart
from their husbands' lines of work, traveled unaccompanied and
dealt with their own real estate issues.

The real disadvantages for women stemmed from the religious and cultural aspects of life. The strictly patriarchal ancient
Judaism, and later the Hellenistic influence with its deep-seated
prejudices, viewed women as inferior beings. These attitudes
caused early rabbinic Judaism to oppose the education of
women. Fortunately, their efforts to impose these views failed; it
was impossible to fully bar women from education in a society
so devoted to learning. The Bible commands each father to educate his children. If the father did not have a boy, he very often
educated his daughter instead, wishing to obey the command

anyway. Many others disregarded the rabbinical objection even if they had sons, simply because they loved their daughters and wished to give them happiness, and a Jew typical of that time could not disassociate happiness from learning. In Egypt in particular, Jewish women had many privileges and exercised greater freedom than anywhere else in the Jewish world. Maimonides, though originating from the repressive Muslim West, followed the Egyptian customs and encouraged women's education. This is evidenced in some of his judgements.

Divorce rate was very high and from the lists of women who married in Fustat and Cairo at that time, forty-five percent of the women married a second time. Of course, some of these women were widowed, but the number of the divorcees, at least among the younger women, appears to be considerably higher. Any social phenomenon is the result of many factors. One obvious reason for the high divorce rate is that a middle-class society, sensitive to both gossip and to the suffering of women, had the leisure to pursue happiness, unlike many poorer-class societies that struggled for basic survival. One letter claimed that a bad marriage was considered a disgrace, akin to prostitution. It was more dignified to end it, and try again with a compatible partner.

Since the primary goal for betrothal was procreation, a woman who passed the childbearing age did not always remarry. However, there is evidence that many middle-aged men and women did marry, for reasons other than producing children—as a means of avoiding sin, for companionship, for financial security, for a comfortable and well-kept home and—perhaps, much as they tried to conceal such an unseemly idea, simply for love.

MAIMONIDES AND HIS WIFE had two children. The first, a little girl, died young, causing the new husband and father fresh grief. The daughter's exact date of birth and death are not known. His second child was born in 1186. This second child, a son, was named Abraham and would survive to take his father's place, and give him the greatest joy in another human being since his brother David's death.

The love and care Maimonides lavished on his son is reminiscent of the relationship he had with his own father, Rabbi Maimon. He educated the child himself, despite the incredible burden of community responsibilities, medical work and writing. Abraham turned out to be worthy of both his father and grandfather. Brilliant and well educated, and raised as the son of a famous father, he nevertheless grew up to be modest, kind and compassionate. Later in life, as the nagid of the Jewish community in Fustat, a writer and a doctor, he was much loved and respected by everyone.

A fragment of a letter written by Maimonides is noteworthy for its illumination of the depth of his feeling about the boy. It was written when Abraham was in his teens:

> Indeed, when I am looking at the state of the world today, I have only two comforts: being involved in some intellectual pursuit or research, and [knowing] that the Lord, may he be praised, gave my son Abraham such grace and blessings that match those of the one he was named after.[2] And he who believes in Him and His Name, would believe in His gifts— may He continue to lengthen his life and his years, as he is humble and modest, in addition to his other good qualities, and possesses a sharp intellect and a beautiful nature, and he will have a great name, undoubtedly, with the help of the Lord. I pray to the Lord, may He be praised, to look after him and complete his kindness.[3]

# 14

## Physician to the Sultan's Court

Every man is the builder of a temple, called his body.
—*Henry David Thoreau*

MAIMONIDES' PRACTICE GREW, and so did his income and his reputation as a physician. People began to recognize him in the street. Jews did not ride horses, but Maimonides replaced his donkey by a handsome mule—a status symbol no renowned physician, or one aspiring to be, did without in Egypt. Maimonides' tall, strong figure looked austere and impressive in his white outfit, riding the fine animal through the throng. He never resorted to the flashy clothes and gimmicky astrological ornaments some of the other doctors tried to impress their patients with.

The real breakthrough in his medical career came in 1187. El Fadil, Saladin's vizier and the most influential man in Egypt, fell ill. The illness, though not life-threatening, prevented him from working, and being a true workaholic he could not abide such restrictions. None of the advice of the court physicians helped any, and El Fadil decided they were all fools and searched for a new physician to get him back on his feet.[1]

Abu Almaali, Maimonides' brother in law, worked as secretary to one of the most important wives of Saladin, possibly the mother of the Al Afdal, the man who would eventually inherit the throne. Abu Almaali had many friends in Saladin's court, and through their influence, El Fadil invited Maimonides to court to discuss a possible health regimen. El Fadil liked Maimonides on first sight and the regimen Maimonides skillfully prescribed worked—and quickly enough to satisfy even El Fadil. Delighted to be able to resume his devastating work schedule, El Fadil appointed Maimonides as court physician. This important position required being entered into the official "Register of Physicians," and it paid an annual salary. The position enhanced the reputation of the doctor and increased his private practice considerably and he was soon to become one of the most respected court physicians.

El Fadil was a powerful, interesting personality. Born in Ascalon, Palestine, and an extremely well-educated man, he also was a wonderful writer and a celebrated master of style. Physically, El Fadil was small, thin and extraordinarily energetic. The amount of work he could accomplish amazed his associates: people claimed he could be giving an audience, writing a letter and simultaneously dictating two other letters to his scribes; all the work was accomplished with compulsive perfectionism.

El Fadil advised several Fatimid rulers before he started working for Saladin. However, he formed an unusual bond with Saladin, and the two men shared complete trust and full understanding, even personal friendship. Their similar Orthodox religious views, tempered by enlightened understanding of other religions, enhanced the relationship. El Fadil gave inestimable help to Saladin with his political and educational reforms. Financially, Saladin rewarded him amply and El Fadil became a very wealthy man. Knowing El Fadil's love of books, Saladin gave his friend the entire Fatimid library, an enormous collection taken from the deposed ruler. On another occasion, Saladin gave El Fadil a gift of another huge library of rare manuscripts obtained as loot during the wars.

Saladin did not stay often in Cairo, and devoted most of his time to campaigns in other countries. Even when away, however, he brought tremendous growth to Egypt, particularly Cairo, Fustat and Alexandria. Saladin built not only the Cairo citadel and many public buildings, but also schools, called the Medressa.

Minaret seen from outside the courtyard of the Mosque of Al-Hakim.

*Below:* Mosque of Sayyidna al-Husayn. Built by the Fatimids, renovated by the Ayyubids. This minaret was probably completed in 1237. It is the shrine to al-Husayn, a descendent of Muhammad and heir to the caliph's throne. He was killed in battle in 680 and his head was brought to Cairo in 1153 for burial.

They were specialized mosques, formed after a Persian model, where various free lectures and courses of study were given. El Fadil, who loved the Medressa, even founded one at his own expense.

Maimonides liked El Fadil, and the friendship between the two men grew to be genuine and enduring. He wrote that El Fadil devoted his life to caring, defending and protecting his people, and generously shared his good fortune with them. He spent much of his wealth to help the poor and educate the needy, ransom prisoners, enlarge the number of academies and help scholars. Maimonides also highly praised El Fadil's excellent writing, public speeches and stylistic ability. He particularly admired his diplomatic skills that saved many a volatile situation.

Since he became court physician, many of the noble Muslim families used Maimonides' medical services. Invariably, they were satisfied with his treatment. Maimonides became not only a famous physician, but acquired the reputation of a doctor who treated not only the body, but the soul as well.

His fame spread to such an extent that certain problems arose. People started blaming Maimonides for his supposed arrogance when he had no time to respond immediately to letters or spend time with visitors. A typical clash of this nature occurred when Abdallatif, a young scholar and doctor of very high reputation, took a trip from Baghdad to Fustat for the sole purpose of hearing Maimonides lecture. He even wrote a poem in his honor. After staying for a while, Abdallatif decided that he did not like Fustat, but entered the service of Saladin anyway, and expected to spend much time with Maimonides. Maimonides was too busy to extend the full hospitality Abdallatif expected, though he probably did wish to see him as he loved meeting other scholars. Abdallatif was extremely offended, and wrote that Maimonides, while trying to please only the great princes, treated his colleagues with arrogance.

A revealing piece of personal testimony is found in a letter by Maimonides written to his trusted disciple Joseph ben Aknin (for whom he composed *The Guide of the Perplexed*) in which he describes his medical practice, his professional responsibilities and his intellectual concerns, and is a good example of his integrity and spirit:

> I inform you that I have acquired in medicine a very good reputation among the great, such as Chief Qadi, the princes, . . . and grandees for whom I do not ordinarily receive any fee. As for the ordinary people, I am placed too high for them to reach me. This obliges me continually to waste my day in Cairo visiting the [noble] sick. When I return to Fustat, the most I am able to do, for the rest of the day and night, is to study medical books, which are so necessary for me. For you know how long and difficult this art is for a conscientious and exact man who does not want to state anything which he cannot support by argument and without knowing where it has been said and how it can be demonstrated. This has further resulted in the fact that I find no time to study Torah; the only time I am able to read the Bible is on Saturday. As for other sciences, I have no time to study them at all and this distresses me very much. Recently I received Averröes' commentaries on Aristotle . . . and my impression is that he explicates the author's views properly, but I have not yet found the time to read all his books.

King Richard the Lionhearted, when staying in Palestine, heard about Maimonides and offered him the position of his personal physician. Maimonides declined. Like his father before him, he did not feel comfortable in Christian lands and preferred to stay in El Fadil's service. Many years later, Ibn abi Usaibia, the historian and physician, bragged in his book, *History of Arabic Physicians*, that he studied under the great Moses Maimonides, and described Maimonides as the man who occupied the highest position of all physicians of his time, in theoretical as well as practical medicine. High praise indeed from the man who became the celebrated head of the great hospital in Cairo. Abraham, Maimonides' son, eventually held a distinguished position in that same hospital.

A truly excellent doctor, Maimonides took his work very seriously. He disliked superstitions of any kind, Muslim and Jewish alike. He rejected all quackery and magical use of amulets, and disdained "sympathetic healing."[2] He strongly objected to those rabbis who claimed that a patient could only be healed through God and considered medical science evil. Maimonides believed that natural resources were good, moral and God-given, studied them extensively, and tested all medicines; he always saw medicine as a science.

Some of Maimonides' views sound curiously modern and his medical writings constitute a significant chapter in the history of medical science. He wanted a doctor to be open to new ideas and research, and believed in moderation, cleanliness and careful diet. He advised proper rest (at night only—he objected to naps during the day) and exercise. He approved of sports, but only as a means to good health, and never as an end in itself. He felt relaxation of mind and body were important, and strongly objected to excess in anything—food, wine or sex. His strong disapproval of excess of any sort included laziness and luxury, considering them unhealthy. The training of the soul toward mental health went hand-in-hand with the training of the body toward physical well being: this was the means to subdue one's cravings for material pleasures that could lead toward sin.

The more he immersed himself in his work, the more it acquired the glow of a sacred duty. Medicine grew akin to ethics, interwoven in his mind to such an extent that in much of his writing they were completely mixed. The Jewish "Physician's Prayer" is attributed to him. We have no ironclad proof he was the author, but most scholars agree that it is very likely, because of many similarities with his other writing and with his style of thinking:

> I am preparing myself to engage in my art; help me, God, in my work, so I shall succeed. Fill my heart with love for my art and for those you have created, and don't let greed and the ambition for glory and honor to mix with my work—because these traits are in contrast with the love of truth and

the love of people. Therefore I ask you: do not mislead me in my great work for the benefit of those you have created. Strengthen the powers of my body and soul so I will always be ready to help the rich and the poor, the good and the bad, the friend and the foe; so that I will always see only the human being in the patient. In the heart of my patients, put faith in me and my knowledge, so that they will listen to my advice and follow my orders. Remove from their sick bed all witch doctors, the army of advisors, and clever quacks—they are a cruel throng, and with their ravings and conceit would negate all good intentions. Let my heart listen to the real wise people, those colleagues who wish to give me wisdom— because it is a big and wide field of study. Strengthen me and give my heart courage against self-deluded fools who fault me—so I will never move away from the way of truth.[3]

Despite Maimonides' protestation in his letter to his disciple that his duties obliged, "[him] continually to waste [his] day in Cairo visiting the [noble] sick," Maimonides was honored by the distinction of serving as physician to the court, and not only took on the extra work willingly, but even enjoyed it. Mingling with the Royal Family, court officials and the noble Muslim families came naturally to him, with his impeccable manners and patrician upbringing.

However, to a man of Maimonides' moral judgement and ethical standards, his first exposure to the inner life of the harem, was morally unsettling. The women of the harem lived in bewildering luxury, spent their days in enforced laziness and their mental and physical states were everything Maimonides vehemently disapproved of. While some of the royal wives had certain administrative duties in the harem, the concubines were treated as playthings, valued only for their beauty and sexual appeal. The eunuchs also repelled him—Jews viewed castration as an abomination. However, he was able to overcome his feelings of repulsion and concentrate on treating each individual as a patient only, as stated in the "Physician's Prayer."

And, inside the Sultan's palace, Maimonides did find a little stolen time for himself. El Fadil's and later, Al Afdal's libraries were always opened to him, and he wrote many of his medical treatises in the palace. For short periods of time he could hide there from his demanding private practice and from the mounting demands from members of the Jewish congregation. He could think and meditate in peace in these quiet, shady, undisturbed rooms, full of beautiful and rare texts.

He also found another strange opportunity for his meditations. His mule quickly learned the way to Cairo in the morning, and back to Fustat at night, and Maimonides did not have to concentrate on following the road. Naturally, he fell to thinking about his studies and his writing. It felt much like going back to his childhood, when he rode with his family, wandering through Andalusia and studying the Torah with Rabbi Maimon. Realizing how much thinking and pre-writing he did in the saddle, and how comfortable he felt doing it, astonished Maimonides. Who would have thought that nostalgia could evolve from such a difficult time—who could really fathom the human mind?

# 15

# The Nagid

*Do not unto others as you would not have them do unto you.*
*That is the whole Law. The rest is commentary—go study.*
*—Hillel the Elder*

AT THIS POINT, the community saw no reason to continue post-poning the inevitable. As early as 1175, many viewed Maimonides as the undisputed authority on Jewish law, and left the determination of many rabbinical legal problems in his hands. In 1177, when he was officially made rabbi, many already saw Maimonides as the unofficial head of the Egyptian Jews. After completing the *Mishneh Torah* in 1180, Maimonides was internationally recognized as the chief authority of the entire Jewish world. Shortly after Maimonides became court physician, the Jewish community bestowed the highest honor on him. In 1187, Maimonides received the title of nagid. He would serve in this position for the rest of his life, and pass the office on to his son Abraham, and on to many future generations of the Maimon family.

The office proved to be a mixed blessing. On one hand, the honor and the happiness of serving the community to the utmost of his ability filled Maimonides' heart with a sense of accomplishment and pride. Knowing that as long as he and his descendants lived, the high office would be safe from the filthy hands of pretenders such as Zuta, and the community would not suffer from their abuse or be demoralized, added to his joy.

On the other hand, the political and judicial governing of the entire Jewish community in Egypt, on top of the time-consuming medical duties, threatened to develop into a heavy burden. Maimonides' constitution was still strong enough to bear the strain, but every so often the old heart problem bothered him. The prospect of so much work frightened him for a short while, and he did occasionally comlpain that the pressures of his many duties robbed him of peace and undermined his health. But he never fell to self-pity, nor did any of his work suffer from the additional burden and he continued writing as prolifically and with the same zeal, and sense of mission, as marked his earlier days of writing.

One of his first rulings as the nagid was in defense of women. Many women were victimized by unscrupulous men, who wished to marry them, take their property and then desert them. Foreign Jews, who already had established families in other countries, further complicated the situation. Maimonides decided to regulate marriages. He decreed that marriages and divorces could only be performed by appointed judges. A foreign Jew could only marry in Egypt if he swore on the Torah to the judge that he was not married before. Once married, if the foreign Jew had to leave the country, he had to fill out a bill of divorcement which became valid after an agreed upon deadline. These regulations prevented many women's lives from being destroyed; Maimonides would continue improving their lot for his entire life.

At times, his judgements regarding the rights of women were so advanced, they created an uproar. He was particularly concerned with poor or disadvantaged women. There are records of a Jewish bachelor who bought a young Christian woman as a slave, converted her to Judaism and lived with her in the house of his father, stepmother and their three children. Islamic laws stated that a Christian could convert only to Islam, and some zealous individuals reported the couple to the Islamic courts. In court, the girl stated that though sold as a Christian, she really was the daughter of a Jewish mother, and therefore Jewish herself. The Islamic authorities accepted her statement, and turned the unpleasant situation over to Maimonides—probably with a sigh of relief.

The dilemma proved a difficult one for Maimonides, because

according to strict Jewish law, anyone who lived illicitly with a woman was forbidden to marry her. Maimonides deliberated: What would the girl's fate be if he stuck to the Law? First, he considered the emotional situation. Jewish families of the time were very close and loving. Turning the girl out might cause a heartbreak not only for the couple but also for the father and stepmother, who very likely embraced her as a daughter, and their three children who would have regarded her as their aunt. Second, what if the girl were pregnant? What would be the fate of her fatherless child? Third, where was the girl to go? As a former slave, she was a displaced person and had no family. Her religious affiliation, which controlled her status in many ways, was at best doubtful.

Maimonides reached the conclusion that turning the girl away would be a senseless cruelty. She had done little to cause the situation. Maimonides' humanity, his common sense and his general acceptance and understanding of human nature revolted against such rigid judgment. As for the young man, who was really responsible for the situation, mending one's ways and living an orderly Jewish life would be more beneficial than punishment by strict law.

Maimonides went back to court and commanded the young man to emancipate the slave girl at once, marry her immediately and mind his ways from that day on. When the court gave a unanimous gasp of shock and disapproval, Maimonides used his sense of humor to relieve the situation. He cited an old saying of the sages as his precedent: "Pay regard to God by disregarding His Law." The tactic worked. The community accepted the judgment without further argument, and the girl glided out of history and into, one hopes, a happy life as a free Jewish woman. The judgment, however, did not fade into history. It served as precedent to help other women in the same situation.

Another story shows clearly that Maimonides had a special regard for women of learning, despite various misconceptions on the subject.

A woman arranged the marriage of one of her sons to a relative, a nine-year-old girl, who had a share of the house in which they all lived. The mother financially maintained the couple for seven years, and then could no longer afford it. By that time, the girl gave birth to a boy, but the husband, who had no wish to support them, abandoned his family and started to travel around the world. He came back once, still without any money or intention to support his family, and stayed long enough to father another child. He never worked and when the second son was a year and a half, he left again for a few more years.

By the age of twenty-five, the wife realized she had to do something for herself and their children. The one favor her husband did for her was to teach her how to read the Bible, and she continued to study on her own for pleasure, and improved her education a great deal. She consulted her brother, a schoolteacher, and he suggested that she should join him as a partner and they would open a school together. They continued to work together for six years, and eventually, when the brother had to leave town, the young woman ran the school herself for about four years. Sometime during these years, the husband came back, and lived with his mother. He never worked and never gave his wife or children any money. The teacher lived with her sons on the school premises, and employed her eldest son, who was by now a teenager, as her associate, so that he could speak to the fathers of the schoolchildren while she spoke with their mothers.

At some point, the husband decided to take the teacher to court. Two letters sent from the couple to Maimonides, who served as the judge, survive in the Cairo Geniza. In the husband's letter, he complains that it hurt his dignity to have his wife working as a teacher, because she had to meet with the fathers of her schoolchildren. Also, he had no one to give him the services of a wife, both conjugal duties and housekeeping. He wanted the teacher to stop working and stay with him. If not, he wished to take a second wife. He did not seek a divorce.

The teacher responds by saying that she cannot leave the school to her son alone, since the parents do not send their children to the school for the teaching of the young man, but for her own teaching. If her husband does not interfere with her school work, the letter continues, she is willing to live with him again, either in her apartment in the family house or on the school premises, and if they stay in the school she is even willing to let him rent the family apartment and take the money for himself. If this is not agreeable, she would be willing to accept a divorce. She refuses to give him permission to take another wife.

Maimonides saw through these letters immediately. Obviously, the husband was irresponsible and lazy, and never fulfilled his obligations. He wanted a woman to be there for his needs, but divorcing his estranged wife would not be acceptable, as she would receive her share in the family home, and take it with her. That was why the husband wanted instead to marry a second wife. Maimonides answered the man officially and formally. By Law, a man was not permitted to marry a second wife without the consent of his first wife. The husband could not, therefore, marry another woman. The teacher must be instructed by the local judge that the husband had the right to request that she stop teaching, and she could not use it as grounds for divorce. This left the husband in exactly the same position as he was before.

To the teacher Maimonides wrote differently, advising her on what he thought was best for her. His advice was quite different from what is to be expected from a patriarchal, Orthodox medieval male. First, he outlined the circumstances, one by one. The husband had the right to forbid her to teach if she lived with him, so if she decided to do that, she would have no means to support herself. If she did live with him, and he could not support her, the husband would be forced, according to Law, to not only release her, but pay her a divorce settlement. However, if she initiated the separation by making the official declaration that "[I cannot] live with this man" and wanted a divorce, she would lose the divorce settlement. Chances were, though, that she would never get the money anyway—this unworthy husband would never meet his obligations. Following this outline, Maimonides suggested she go boldly ahead and request a divorce. As a divorced woman, she could teach what she liked to anyone she liked, and would have disposition over herself. The woman followed the unexpected, un-Orthodox suggestion, and chose freedom.

THE YEAR 1187 CONTINUED to be eventful and significant. Saladin won victory over the Christians re-conquering most of Palestine from the Crusaders. Jerusalem, under Christian rule for over eighty years, returned to the hands of the Muslims. Maimonides used his influence, and Saladin generously agreed to invite the Jews to come back to Jerusalem and also settle freely throughout Palestine. This gave Maimonides, always emotionally attached to Palestine, great joy. Not long after, a most unexpected and extremely dangerous situation arose. Maimonides came closer to execution than even in Fez, and strangely enough, the cause was his old friend Abul Arab ibn Moisha, the same man who saved his life in Fez.

Abul Arab ibn Moisha came to Egypt on business to find Maimonides possessing the highest title in the Jewish community. It shocked Ibn Moisha, for in Fez, he honestly believed that Maimonides truly adopted the faith of Islam. Maimonides never converted, but like many of his brethren lived the double life of feigning acceptance of Islam and disguising his ways in public as far as possible to appear like Muslims, while practicing Judaism in the privacy of his home. Ibn Moisha was fooled and under this delusion, he risked his own life to intervene when the authorities intended to execute Maimonides after his friend, Rabbi Judah ibn Shoshan, was arrested as a practicing Jew and found guilty and then executed. When Ibn Moisha encountered Maimonides in Egypt, thinking Maimonides had converted to Islam in Fez, he assumed he had now relapsed and reverted to Judaism. Ibn Moisha was furious about what he perceived as a betrayal of both his faith and friendship—angry enough to report Maimonides to the authorities. According to Muslim law, if a man converted to Islam and then returned to his own faith, he faced execution. Ibn Moisha demanded that Maimonides be put before a tribunal. Fortunately, El Fadil headed the tribunal.

El Fadil was a good and faithful Muslim, not a thoughtless

fanatic. He already knew and greatly admired Maimonides, and did not intend to lose his friend and trusted physician over a technicality. But the law was the law, and for a while the danger hung over Maimonides' head while El Fadil frantically tried to come up with a solution to the dilemma. In the end, he decided to simply follow the truth. He declared that Maimonides never really adopted the faith or converted but only kept a fabulous disguise, and therefore, could not have had a relapse. The charges were officially dropped and Maimonides was exonerated.

Saved from danger, Maimonides concentrated on his work. His fears regarding the degree of overwork were justified but despite the growing demands on his time and his growing fame as a physician, he never stopped studying medicine; insisting that a doctor required lifelong study. He also was often functioning as a judge. As nagid, the number of inquiries from every corner of the Jewish world doubled. Letters came from rabbis, judges, scholars, students, teachers, heads of schools, and even many private citizens sent their letters and expected an official responsum. Maimonides replied to every letter. He did not like employing a secretary, fearing that having such an assistant might make him seem arrogant. He preferred answering his own letters, and made a point of answering every single one for the rest of his life, except when too sick to write. Many of the letters found in the Cairo Geniza and in other places bear his well-known personal signature. He did not answer everyone automatically and with the same degree of detail—scholars and officials received detailed responsa—common people received a simple letter. All, however, were answered with the same politeness, compassion, authority and enlightenment. Many of his answers were collected, copied and sent to various communities. People who copied the *Mishneh Torah* sent him the copies to check for accuracy and sign—each time, a monumental job to accomplish.

Despite, or perhaps because of the growing honor paid to Maimonides, the opposition grew just as strongly. The *Mishneh Torah* was hailed as the greatest book since the Mishna was completed by Rabbi Judah ha-Nasi, Maimonides' ancestor. While spreading his fame, the *Mishneh Torah* nevertheless aroused tremendous criticism. Maimonides took the opposition very well. He sometimes admitted that the opposers were correct, thanked them for their criticism and requested that they should continue the examination of his work and find more problems for him to correct. He never claimed infallibility, or wished to become an authority written in stone.

Of peculiar interest was the attitude of the heads of communities. Jews were self-governing in most of the Muslim world. They had a "nasi" in Palestine, the "exilarch" in Syria, the "resh galuta" in Persia and the "nagid" in Egypt. The Talmud served as the book of Laws, and was not well understood by the masses. By using the *Mishneh Torah*, the layman could easily understand the Law, and some of the leaders were not entirely happy about this.

A particularly difficult situation occurred in Baghdad, where *two* officials functioned as heads of the Jewish community. The exilarch Daniel dealt with political matters, and would select judges, rabbis and heads of community. The gaon Samuel ben Ali dealt with spiritual matters only. Unfortunately, Samuel ben Ali was a good scholar, but far from being a spiritual man. He was extremely wealthy, kept sixty slaves and lived in a palace near Baghdad, surrounded by immense gardens. His daughter, a celebrated genius, shared her immense Bible and Talmud scholarship by delivering lectures to students. As they were all young men, she lectured while hidden from view, thus maintaining her modesty.

In 1175, the exilarch Daniel died. He had no son, and two of his nephews battled for the exilarchate. The state of chaos allowed Samuel ben Ali to seize power in both religious and judicial matters, and try to combine the two offices. He appointed officials, rabbis and judges on his own authority, and took control of the community's finances. The Muslim authorities began to acknowledge him, and his seal of the "Gaon of Baghdad" carried official power. Even after another exilarch was finally chosen, Samuel ben Ali refused to give up the advantages he felt were his due.

Samuel and Maimonides had a long-standing feud. Since the

gaon considered the college in Baghdad the head of all Jewish authority, he naturally saw Maimonides as a dangerous rival. Maimonides never hid his disapproval of the luxury in which the geonim of Baghdad conducted their lives, and challenged their supremacy. In addition, Samuel ben Ali disliked Maimonides' innovative attitude and advanced views, so different from his own conservative approach. The strongest opposition to the *Mishneh Torah* came from the Ben Ali camp and contemporary scholars claim that Samuel ben Ali and his associates actually refused to read the *Mishneh Torah*, because they were afraid that rumors would claim that they studied it for their own benefit. Worse, they spread rumors that Maimonides (who by this time was already being recognized as a pillar of the traditional faith) was neither a strictly religious Jew, nor a follower of the Talmud.

Maimonides took it well, and did not fight back. He said that it was not necessary to vanquish fools, only to avoid them. He had no need to win a victory, but only to teach those who were fit to be taught. Still, the strain was immense, and after the worst skirmish was over he became quite ill, as he always did during a period of great strain or after a terrible blow.

Jewish leaders in the Christian countries did not find the book so threatening. They were very interested in it as a study guide, and received it well, with the exception of Rabbi Abraham ben David of Posquières,[1] who was not entirely satisfied with the book and decided to examine it. However, although he used some strong language in his criticism, he intended no personal enmity, and viewed the material objectively. Today, Rabbi Abraham's comments are sometimes printed together with the *Mishneh Torah*, in addition to the comments of Rabbi Joseph Karo. It is amusing that the *Mishneh Torah*, which Maimonides created for the purpose of simplifying the Law and relieving it of commentaries, attracted commentaries and discussions of its own.

# 16

## The Guide of the Perplexed

Books must be read as deliberately and
reservedly as they were written.
—*Henry David Thoreau*

THE GUIDE OF THE PERPLEXED[1] is one of the most influential texts
in Judaism and constituted what most scholars consider a major
contribution to the "accomodation between science, philosophy
and religion." Translated into Latin it also found its way to many
non-Jewish schools of thought, influencing the great medieval
scholastic writers and inspiring important philosophers, such as
Benedict de Spinoza, Albertus Magnus, G.W. Leibniz and
Thomas Aquinas. *The Guide* was written as a special gift for a single human being. The man who served as a catalyst for this monumental, enduring work was Maimonides' student and protégé.

Joseph ibn Aknin was a young man who lived in Ceuta, the
same port city in Morocco Maimonides and his family spent
some time in just before escaping to Palestine. An extremely
well-educated man, Joseph studied mathematics, science, philosophy and medicine in addition to the usual Judaic studies. For a
while he studied philosophy with Averroës. Joseph wrote very
well, and was the first to compose *makamas*, tales in rhyme in the
tradition of Arab poets, into Hebrew. His great love was philosophical theology. When he first he heard of Maimonides,
Joseph was engaged in interpreting the *Song of Songs* according
to its hidden, metaphorical meaning.

The double life of the pseudo convert to Islam caused Joseph a great deal of mental suffering. In 1185, when the connection between the two men began, conditions in Morocco had deteriorated further than in Maimonides' short stay there. In 1184, Abd al Mumin died, and the new ruler, Al Mansur, persecuted both the Jews and the converts. He subjected them to various forms of harassment, and even forced them to wear special garments—a black cloak with wide sleeves that hung low to the ground, and a yellow veil instead of a turban. Joseph ben Aknin, a proud and sensitive man, found these conditions extremely humiliating. Joseph had reached an intellectual impasse; he felt unsuccessful in combining religion and philosophy as well as he wanted and was struggling with these issues when copies of the *Mishneh Torah* reached Ceuta.

Every page contained a stunning revelation. The more Joseph pored over the book, the more he felt the writer would be the one teacher he so desperately needed. He dreamed of leaving Morocco and traveling to Egypt to meet Maimonides but he knew he could not go directly to Egypt, a country that allowed freedom to Jews. The Moroccan authorities, who knew Joseph as a converted Jew, would have suspected him of relapsing back to Judaism. But he could go to Spain, where he was not known and from there take the boat to Alexandria. With a sudden determination, Joseph gave up his medical practice and caught a boat to Spain.

When he reached Alexandria, he could not bring himself to go to Fustat, feeling it might be an imposition. Instead, he wrote to Maimonides, explaining his wish to study with him, and also sent him some poems. Maimonides, not particularly interested in poetry, could not fail to see that the poet nevertheless wrote very well. The style of the letters showed him a man of great learning and rare intellect. This represented a luxury being that Egypt did not have a large number of true scholars. During his entire adult life, Maimonides missed the atmosphere of great learning he had known in Spain, and felt slightly isolated in his adopted country. (The congregations in France and Babylon offered better scholars, but Maimonides did not have either the time or the inclination for much travel.) This is probably why references to "back home in Andalusia" so often appear wistfully in his writing. He promptly invited the young man to visit. They met and formed an instant friendship that lasted until the end of Maimonides' life. Maimonides accepted the brilliant young man as his disciple, and set him on a regular course of studies.

In the beginning, Joseph was ecstatic about the association, but naturally, they soon had their intellectual clashes. Joseph wanted to be instructed quickly in the deeper Torah mysteries, while Maimonides believed in a slow and meticulous advancement, with serious preparation for each step. He gave Joseph careful attention, and in addition to his usual studies, engaged him in working on astronomical matters that interested both men. When material about prophecy or Torah mysteries came up, Maimonides explained them, but neither delved deeply nor continued further than the matter at hand. Joseph was frustrated, but these differences did not interfere with the understanding between the two scholars. Joseph did not entirely fill the void David left in Maimonides' heart—no one could do that—but the companionship of the brilliant young man gave him more happiness than Maimonides expected to ever find in another person.

Joseph became a close friend not only to Maimonides, but to his family and his entourage as well. Much more than a mere disciple, he assisted Maimonides in many ways in Fustat, and occasionally traveled on his behalf. It was soon after his arrival that Maimonides' son Abraham was born, and the jubilant Maimonides, holding his first boy in his arms after all these years, told Joseph that he is viewed them both as his beloved sons.

They spent two years studying together. For various business reasons that remain a mystery, Joseph could not stay in Egypt and in 1187 was to move to Allepo. There he engaged, quite successfully, in both medicine and business. His business involved frequent travel, and he often went to Baghdad, where he met both the exilarch and the gaon Samuel ben Ali. Eventually he moved to Baghdad and would remain there permanently.

The association between teacher and disciple, however, was far from ended. They corresponded a great deal, and it was Joseph's departure that planted the seed for Maiomides' classic masterpiece in religious philosophy, *The Guide of the Perplexed*, which he was to labor on for fifteen years and would see translated into Hebrew in his lifetime and later into Latin and most European languages. In the introduction to the book, which is written as a personal letter to Joseph, Maimonides explaines that he had formed his good opinion of him on his early letters from Alexandria, that he rose in his estimate when they studied together and that as they had to part, he would continue to teach him by sending him the book as he composed it, chapter by chapter. In addition, he hoped the book would serve others like Joseph, people who were well versed in the Law and in philosophy, but were perplexed by the seeming conflict between the two, and by many allegorical expressions in the Bible.

Maimonides' love of philosophy is evidenced by his extensive, lifelong study of the works of the Jewish as well as the Arab and Hellenistic philosophers, particularly Aristotle. Deeply Jewish as he was himself, Maimonides believed that all great philosophers shared a basic truth, regardless of their religious background. In the *The Guide of the Perplexed* he showed that Judaism is the true expression of human intelligence, and nothing in its literature really contradicts true philosophy. Within medieval Judaism, Nathan N. Glatzer says in his *Judaic Tradition*, Maimonides "made the most determined attempt to do justice to both faith and knowledge." He paid for this open-minded attitude with tremendous scandals and opposition, but never deviated from his convictions. His heart and mind told him that universal science and religion are one and the same.

The organization of the book is not as clear and straightforward as the division of his other books. This was deliberate. Maimonides regarded the book as dangerous to many who were not qualified to understand it, and created a system of precautions that concealed many of his true thoughts. He explained in his introduction that he wrote every word with extreme care, so one had to read just as carefully if one wished to understand the book's structure and the meaning.

The book deals with esoteric subjects such as the nature of God, including His incorporeality, and the problem of the anthropomorphic description of God in the Bible; the nature of Creation and the Creation as Prime Causes. Miracles, the question of evil or its absence, the purpose of life, Providence, Prophecy and the intelligence of the Spheres are all discussed in detail as well. He deals with the mysteries of the Chariot, an important part of Jewish metaphysics; and he compares the Kalam, a Muslim philosophy, to Aristotelian philosophy. Some of the wisdom of these systems he accepted, some he rejected. He also returned to the positive and negative Precepts he originally discussed in *Sefer ha-Mitzvot*. *The Guide* is a treasure trove of not only questions that have occupied the minds of thinking people since the beginning of inquiry—but also answers. Some of Maimonides' interpretations are in line with the sages of the Talmud and Mishna. Some are entirely original, and even contradict their opinions.

*The Guide* generated tremendous interest very quickly. Many more people were reading it than Maimonides expected would and those special readers for whom the book was intended fell in love with it. Religious scholars who were also philosophers saw his line of reasoning and could finally reconcile the differences that prayed on their minds. In Provence, France, the book became a huge success. Provence's sages wrote Maimonides to request a copy in Hebrew, if possible, since they could not read Arabic, and if this could not be had, they would take an Arabic copy and have his book translated. Maimonides had no time to translate his book and sent them a copy in Arabic. They chose Samuel ibn Tibbon, himself a scholar and the son of another well-known scholar, to be the translator of the work. Ibn Tibbon wrote Maimonides to request the needed permission.

Maimonides, who was familiar with the work of Samuel ibn

Tibbon's father, was delighted with the sages' choice. He wrote Samuel that he was honored that the son of such a valued scholar chose to translate his work. Maimonides gave him advice about the translation that should go into current textbooks and benefit modern translators. Maimonides advised him not to bother to follow each word slavishly. Rather, the translator must be sure that the thought is clear and understandable, and transmit that thought, even if some words or phrases must be changed or even omitted. Above all, Maimonides added, a good translation must be clear, interesting and more than a copy of the original. It must be a new creation.

Ibn Tibbon was well qualified to do the job, but after completing three sections, he sent a copy to Maimonides for revision. He would not feel comfortable, he wrote, until he knew he was transmitting Maimonides' thoughts properly. Maimonides approved and Ibn Tibbon finished the job. The translation succeeded beyond expectations, and was scholarly and accurate; other translators did not do so well. The famous poet Judah al Harizi, tried and failed. Scholars, including Maimonides' son Abraham, did not like Al Harizi's translation. Abraham felt it was full of mistakes and omissions, and Ibn Tibbon himself criticized the translation, not because he objected to competition, but because it was not scholarly. He said that Al Harizi could accomplish the translation of light fiction and verse, but no more.

The popularity of the book frightened Maimonides. He never expected it, and he was afraid it might serve as an excuse for new persecutions of the Jews. But this never happened. Arab philosophy was influenced by it, and Christians studied it. However, it was in Jewish circles that *The Guide* became the center of the greatest controversy generated by Maimonides, a controversy that lasted well after his death. While some philosophers felt it was the most influential Jewish book since the Torah, and that introducing Hellenism into Judaism was a magnificent attempt at unifying knowledge, others condemned it as heresy.

Quite a few rabbis simply resented the introduction of anything relating to paganism into Judaism. Some felt that it actually encouraged young people to turn to Hellenism and away from traditional and rabbinic Judaism. Others, perhaps strangely enough to the modern reader, objected to the stress Maimonides put on the incorporeality of God. One of those who objected, a rabbi who actually loved Maimonides, mourned that the book was written at all. He felt that *The Guide* threatened the Jewish nation, transformed its sacred tradition into fancies—and turned God Himself into a dream.

A SURPRISINGLY FURIOUS opposition, about thirty years after Maimonides' death came from a city in France—Montpellier—from Rabbi Shlomo ben Abraham. He called for a ban on the both the *Mishneh Torah* and *The Guide* and threatened anyone studying either of them with excommunication. Other rabbis in Northern France joined in the official ban as well. The sages of Lunel though stood up in Maimonides' defense. In retaliation, they banned Rabbi Shlomo and his associates, sparking what was to become a holy war, spreading throughout France, across the Pyrenees, into Spain and from there, all over the Jewish world.

When some moderate Jews tried to reconcile the warring factions, an ugly response came from Maimonides' opponents. In 1233, they enlisted the help of the Catholic Church. The rabbis went to the Dominican monks of Paris, and informed them that Maimonides' works endangered not only Judaism, but all religion. The Dominicans obliged their request for some action to be taken. They seized Maimonides' books and burned them at the stake. They arrested those Jews who had read the banned books, and proceeded to try them at court. Some Jews were found guilty and lost their lives. Maimonides' son Abraham defended his father's books, and wrote two important works in their defense. One was in response to the accusations by another rabbi in Montpellier, Scholom Daniel ben Saadia and his supporters, who accused *The Guide of the Perplexed* of being a dangerously heretical book. After this zealot instigated Church authorities in Montpellier to burn copies of the books in 1235, Abraham protested by writing the famous *Wars of the Lord*.

The Jewish world was horrified. Level-headed individuals, such as the philosopher Abraham ben Hasdai and the scholar Samuel Saporta begged the factions to stop the insane warring. They were not heard. Instead, Maimonides' supporters answered with a crime of equal magnitude. They brought the informers against Maimonides to trial, and responded with unholy joy when the authorities found them guilty and cut out their tongues, as was the barbarous medieval custom for the punishment of false witnesses. How mortified Maimonides would have been, had he lived through these "wars of the Lord."

In 1241, Nicholas Donin, a converted Jew who had become a Dominican, led the monks into Jewish homes, seized all the holy books, and burned them. The Jews, looking at the giant bonfire as it consumed their treasured heritage, could not say that they did not lead the way toward the horror.

And still it didn't stop. Around the end of the century, a particularly zealous man, Rabbi Ben Aderet, banned the study of all books except the Bible and the Talmud. The fight between both Maimonides' opposition and his following broke out with renewed strength. Only in 1306, when the Jews were expelled from France with all their property confiscated, did they realize they were all one nation. Most people started reading Maimonides' books for consolation. One man tried to do penance by making a pilgrimage to Maimonides' tomb and died on the way. The tragedy caused the entire Jewish world to believe God's wrath had killed the pilgrim. Ben Aderet later denied that he meant to include Maimonides' books in his ban.

Time passed. With the opposition finally forgotten, *The Guide of the Perplexed* took it's rightful place as the foremost book in Jewish philosophy. An entire library of interpretation, commentary and reviews was written. Thinkers throughout the ages and, not only rabbinic Jews, but even the Karaites continued to follow and be influenced by it. Strangely, the Kabbalists, whose mysticism had nothing in common with Maimonides' rationalism, nevertheless loved and studied *The Guide*.

In the thirteenth century *The Guide of the Perplexed* was translated into Latin, on the request of Frederic II, an enlightened king who admired Jewish learning. The translation found its way to the Christian philosophers Albertus Magnus and Thomas Aquinas. Eventually, even the fierce Dominicans stopped objecting to *The Guide*, and started reading it. The Franciscans found much in common between Maimonides and St. Francis of Assisi. The Christians, by acknowledging the universality of the book, did more for *The Guide of the Perplexed* at that early time than the Jews themselves.

More time passed and Spinosa, Leibniz, Hegel, Mendelssohn and Munk joined the army of admirers and followers of *The Guide*. By the middle of the nineteenth century, it was already translated into numerous European languages.

Fountain at the Mosque of Al-Hakim in Cairo.
(Photo by Mary Knight)

# 17

## The Adversity of Fame

To be great is to be misunderstood.
—*Ralph Waldo Emerson*

THE YEAR 1190 MARKED the momentous achievement of the completion of *The Guide of the Perplexed*, and brought Maimonides a whirlwind of activity. He was not ready. Only fifty-five years old and at the height of his success, he felt as tired as if he had lived twice as long. However, he refused to let physical weariness stop him, and continued to shoulder his enormous load. Fate would have been kinder if his peers and subordinates could have extended unconditional help to the man who nearly killed himself with overwork on their behalf, but this is not how human nature operates, and his opposition took an ugly turn. Much of it centered around the *Mishneh Torah*.

The objection to the *Mishneh Torah* became an absurd phenomenon in Alexandria. A full rebellion broke out against Maimonides in the congregation headed by Rabbi Pinchas ben Meshulam, an old friend and associate of Maimonides. The congregation flatly refused to obey Maimonides and claimed he acted arbitrarily in his judicial decisions. As it often occurred with Maimonides' innovative decisions, this was a matter of custom versus Law.

In Alexandria, the Jews had followed the Islamic custom of washing before praying for so many years, that at that time they believed it a requirement of Jewish law. Reading in the *Mishneh Torah* that they did not need to do so shocked them. At first, Rabbi Pinchas was prepared to accept Maimonides' decision, but the infuriated congregation threatened to fire the poor rabbi. To save himself, Rabbi Pinchas reversed his decision and wrote a most indignant letter to Maimonides. It included the old and tired accusations that the *Mishneh Torah* attempted to displace the Talmud and that it was deficient as a book of laws because it lacked listed sources. It is hard to decide how Rabbi Pinchas really felt about the matter, but he ended up preaching against the book in public.

Maimonides heard these accusations many times, but Rabbi Pinchas was an old friend whose opinion he valued, and the letter came at the wrong moment. Maimonides was very sick at the time and suspected that he was facing death. The attack, therefore, distressed him disproportionately to the situation. Even in his weakened condition he could not be too concerned about the ridiculous bathing question, but the matter of the listed sources began to pray on his mind, and interfered with his recovery.

Just as he began to recover his health and realize that he was not about to die, another unpleasant situation arose, though the person who initiated it meant no harm. A distinguished judge asked Maimonides for help, pointing out that he could not find the source for one of Maimonides' decisions in the *Mishneh Torah*. It had happened before, and until then, Maimonides could always find the necessary source. This time, however, he was horrified to realize that he could not find the source. For a few agonizing hours he made one mistake after another, desperately trying to locate the passage. Eventually he found it, of course, but by then his own faith in himself was shaken to the core—for the first time in his life. He bitterly blamed himself for making the terrible mistake of not listing the sources, and vowed to create a special book listing all the sources as an appendix, sometime in the near future. The knowledge that his memory betrayed him so completely stunned Maimonides.

Then, Samuel ben Ali decided to strike again with a double-pronged attack.

The first item on his agenda regarded the resurrection of the dead. After reading the *Mishneh Torah*, which dealt more with prophecy and the immortality of the soul than with the bodily resurrection of the dead, many people asked Maimonides if he believed that the resurrection of the body was a biblically held belief. Even the Yemenites, a congregation that admired Maimonides almost to adoration, sent him a letter questioning his position about it. Maimonides was in no hurry to do anything about it because he believed he expressed himself clearly enough in the book, and declared he was too busy to repeat himself. However, the enmity and endless persecution from Ben Ali finally convinced Maimonides to pay attention.

A young man named Zecharia became a student of Samuel ben Ali. The well-educated, intelligent young man promptly lost his head. First, he fell in love with Ben Ali's daughter, the celebrated biblical and talmudic scholar who amazed everyone with her genius. Second, he worshiped the gaon himself, dazzled by Ben Ali's power, dignity and wealth, and opulent surroundings. Samuel Ben Ali welcomed the young man, allowed him to marry his daughter and started grooming him for an official position in the future. Years later, after Samuel ben Ali's death, Zecharia became the new gaon.

When Zecharia met Joseph ibn Aknin, he developed an acute dislike for Maimonides' friend and disciple. Topped with the enmity he already felt toward Maimonides on behalf of his father-in-law, a feud resulted. Aided by Samuel ben Ali, Zecharia plunged into a campaign against Maimonides' "heretical" views of the resurrection. The matter took added importance when two scholars, Meir Abulafia of Toledo and Abraham ben David of Pusquières joined the fight against Maimonides. They called for a ban against his books.

The situation escalated into a public debate with letters flying back and forth, all accusing or defending Maimonides of misinterpreting or upholding the biblical view of the Resurrection. Maimonides ignored it, particularly since he considered Zechariah a rather unimportant person. Samuel ben Ali, therefore, decided to become further involved. One Yemenite, not satisfied with Maimonides' silence about the Resurrection, asked Samuel ben Ali about his views. The gaon saw this as an opportunity to fully air his ideas, and wrote a philosophical treatise about the nature of the Resurrection.

There was nothing inappropriate in the gaon writing about his opinions on a religious matter in a formal treatise, but unfortunately, he did not limit himself to that. In the treatise, Ben Ali denounced Maimonides' views, twisting his words and accusing him of heresy. He included some praise for Maimonides, too, to follow the polite custom, but no one could mistake the hostile intention. At the same time, he wrote Maimonides a separate letter, containing both exaggerated flattery and a reproach for making errors in the interpretation of the Talmud. Samuel ben Ali went as far as to offer protection to Maimonides against the angry congregation in Yemen—an obvious attempt to prove his own superiority. For once, Maimonides was furious. He wrote an uncharacteristic angry response, sharply pointing out to Samuel ben Ali his own mistakes. Furthermore, he mentioned the secret attacks Samuel Ben Ali initiated against himself, with the intent of embarrassing ben Ali by the fact that he was informed about his low behavior. Little did he know that Ben Ali simply could not be embarrassed by such trivia. He might have even been proud of his own astuteness.

The feud went on. Samuel ben Ali even tried to drag the exilarch into the fray, but the plot did not succeed. Finally, Maimonides decided to do what he felt he should have done in the first place—ignore Samuel ben Ali. Maimonides was sufficiently self-assured to do this in style, but his protégé Joseph ben Aknin was extremely angry. He felt something had to be done to repair Maimonides' reputation, and considered opening an academy in Baghdad. In such a school, he would teach Maimonides' system, using the *Mishneh Torah* as text. He wrote Maimonides for permission.

Maimonides was touched by his student's devotion. He thought about his idea, which seemed tempting enough, understanding it could help his situation. After much deliberation though, he wrote Joseph a comforting letter, asking him to ignore the libel and the insinuations, which were beneath both Maimonides and Joseph. He reminded Joseph that so many people, once they acquire power, lose their humility and perhaps even their faith, and Ben Ali, so involved with personal power, was likely to suffer such fate. He reminded him, too, that Ben Ali and Zecharia really did have one or two good reasons to dislike Joseph. After all, Joseph supported the choice of an exilarch that Samuel objected to, and had showed open hostility toward Zecharia. There was no reason to expect them to like either Maimonides or Joseph. He then advised Joseph not to open an academy. As a head of an academy, he would have endless conflicts with the gaon, and probably neglect his own business and his medical practice. This would force him to accept a salary from either the exilarch or the gaon, leading to further trouble and aggravation.

He knew, however, that he could no longer ignore the question of the Resurrection. Busy as he was, Maimonides decided to write a response, which resulted in his striking Epistle on Resurrection. He did not write the epistle in his usual calm and composed style; feeling he had explained it all before, his anger shows through in his writing. However, it is as well organized and clear as any of his writing.

In the epistle he explains what caused the confusion that lead to the idea that he denied bodily resurrection. Much of the material in the *Mishneh Torah*, he wrote, dealt more with the world to come, and in this treatise he fully meant to balance it. Then, he repudiated all the allegations against him regarding his personal belief in the Resurrection, and reinforced all arguments with biblical passages. He set out to explain why the Torah does not dwell on physical resurrection and explained how he arrived at his conclusions. Maimonides sent it out and hoped that this would end the matter.

It did not. The debate moved out of the hands of the main participants and groups of people including writers, poets and men of science and great learning, enjoyed themselves tremendously as they carried the raging scholarly debate all over the entire Jewish world and much of the non-Jewish world as well. It still goes on.

The second issue Ben Ali brought against Maimonides again involved custom versus Law, and started innocently enough. Rabbi Abraham ha-Cohen from Baghdad, posing the question to Maimonides wrote: Is it permitted to sail on the great rivers—the Tigris, the Euphrates and the Nile—on Saturday? Maimonides answered that it was permitted, adding a detailed explanation that also showed how the Law supported his views, and suggested to Rabbi Abraham that he should show both question and answer to Samuel ben Ali, as a courtesy, and hear his opinion too.

Maimonides' answer went against the custom in Baghdad, where the Jews did not travel the rivers on Saturday. However, the responsum was based entirely on the Torah. It is never stated in the Torah that traveling the rivers on Saturday is forbidden, and Maimonides decided that in this case, as in all others regarding custom, the decision of how to follow it is up to the individual, unlike matters involving the Law, which must be fully obeyed.

Samuel ben Ali saw Maimonides' answer as trespassing on his authority in Baghdad. He didn't care much about what people did on the Nile, but the Tigris and Euphrates he considered his personal territory. He sent back a letter, very polite and full of praises, but plainly declaring that Maimonides was wrong. Generally, Maimonides took criticism very calmly. He welcomed discussions, and was not insulted even if a student reacted skeptically to his teachings. He saw criticism as helpful, and maintained that anyone can make a mistake. But this was different; Maimonides resented the way the gaon treated him, in public and within his own circle. He knew how much his own words were twisted and corrupted by Samuel ben Ali. His letter of response was polite, cool and very Andalusian, as always. But following the well-mannered introduction, he set out to prove to the gaon how wrong he was, in no uncertain terms. Anyone who read the responsum, and many did, could not deny that Maimonides was right.

It made no difference at all. Samuel ben Ali, jealous and vindictive, continued to forbid sailing the rivers on Saturday.

LIFE IS RARELY ALL grim, and in 1195, a pleasant surprise arrived from Provence. The Jewish sages of the town of Lunel studied the *Mishneh Torah* as carefully as Maimonides could have possibly wished it, and requested permission to ask the author a few questions. Reading the letter filled Maimonides' heart with joy. It was neither a subservient, blind acceptance of the Master's command, nor was it a wild attack on his shortcomings. The spokesman, Jonathan Cohen, wrote an intelligent, gentlemanly and scholarly inquiry, which Maimonides took a great delight in reading and answering. This was the kind of response he craved for his books.

He complimented the sages on the inquiry, telling them only great scholars could have given him such constructive criticism and questions, and begged them to continue to do so, because no one was free from errors and he appreciated their help. Secretly, he rejoiced in the fact that the community in Lunel had no affiliation to the gaon, the exilarch or even to himself as the nagid. Perhaps they were somewhat isolated, but Maimonides knew they constituted a new hope for Judaism in Europe. They reminded him of the congregation in Córdoba.

This correspondence did him a world of good. At that time, Maimonides was recovering from another long illness. He returned to his medical practice, but his heart was badly damaged, his senses a little dimmed and he was very weak. His hands trembled so much he found it hard to write, and had to dictate much of his correspondence. He only reconciled himself to what he thought of as vain luxury, when as secretary, he employed his physician-nephew Abu Alracha. It felt a little less unpleasant when the secretary was his sister's boy, whom he had trained himself. He made sure, however, to answer Rabbi Jonathan's personal part of the letter with his own hand, apologizing to the recipient for not being able to write the whole thing.

At this time, Samuel ibn Tibbon was working on the translation of *The Guide of the Perplexed*. The young man, perfectly qualified to do the job, felt awed by both manuscript and author.

He wanted to be near Maimonides so he could ask him questions, and requested permission to visit him. Maimonides' answer gives us a rare glimpse into his life.

The Lord knows how I have written so much. I run away from people, hiding where they would not notice me, sometimes I lean against a wall, sometimes I lie down to write because my extreme weakness is conspiring with my age.

Regarding your visit—come, and welcome, and I am happy about it and wish, long and yearn for it, and I will have more joy seeing you than you will have seeing me, though it is difficult for me to think about the danger of your coming by sea. I would suggest and advise you not to endanger yourself, because your coming will only allow you to see me, and allow me to honor you as much as I can; but discussing any wisdom or discipline, or even have an hour alone with me, day or night—don't expect that, because my affairs go as I will tell you:

I live in Fustat, and the Sultan resides in Cairo, and between the two places there are two Sabbath zones. The Sultan has a difficult habit—it is impossible for me to avoid seeing him every morning. If he is weak, or if any of his sons or concubines is sick—I cannot leave Cairo, and I spend most of the day in the Sultan's house. It is impossible to avoid seeing his ministers every day, or an official or two may be sick, and I have to take care of their healing. Therefore—every day I go to Cairo at dawn, and if no trouble or anything new happened, I go back to Fustat after at least half a day. When I arrive, quite hungry, I find the parlor full of non Jews, important and unimportant, and judges, and officials, a mixed company; they know when I am expected. I dismount from my beast, wash my hands, and go out to apologize for keeping them waiting a few minutes while I eat a quick meal, often the only meal during the day. Then I go to take care of them and write their prescriptions, and there is coming and going until late at night, and sometimes—may the Torah be my witness—I may be up until two o'clock in the morning. I talk to them lying down from exhaustion, and when the evening is over I can no longer talk. The result is that no man of Israel can speak to me or spend some time with me except on Saturday. They all come after prayer, I guide the community as to what they should do during the week, we have a short reading until noon, and then they leave. Many come back in the afternoon for another reading until the evening prayer.

This is the way my affairs go, and I only told you a little of what you will see with the help of the Lord, blessed be his name. When you complete the translation you have started—since you started the mitzva[1] you should finish it—come for a visit, not for study, because my time is so limited.[2]

But this was not all he had to do. His medical duties involved him in an entirely new direction—extensive medical writing.

Courtyard of the Great Mosque in Córdoba, back in Maimonides' beloved Spain, which he was to refer to throughout his life in his correspondence. (Photo by Gregory Frux)

# 18

# Merging with the Light

Time dissipates to shining ether the solid angularity of facts.
—*Ralph Waldo Emerson*

MANY READERS MIGHT ASSUME that because Maimonides lived eight hundred years ago, his attitude toward medicine would necessarily have been medieval. Therefore, the degree to which his thought process proved scientific and modern may be a surprise. True, he based much of his work on the ancient Greek doctors' writings and he admired the great Arab doctors, but Maimonides never prescribed a single medication that he didn't test himself. He introduced unexpected innovations, including some most astonishing theories on psychosomatic medicine, and he was a great pioneer of preventive medicine. He declared that the goal of medicine was to prevent disease rather than to cure it, and maintained that as preventive measures one must visit the doctor often, even when well, and live an orderly, well-regulated life. This way, one could avoid sickness before it attacks. It is not surprising then that some of the wealthy and noble patients, who thought very highly of him, asked him to write treatises on specific subjects.

How he found the time to do it is a mystery, but somehow Maimonides obliged these requests. Maimonides was often too sick and the trembling of his hands prevented him from writing, requiring his nephew Abu Alracha to take dictation. But the books were invariably concise and beautifully organized; the busy physicians who read them did not have to waste time looking for specific information. The medical treatises became extremely popular, and were translated into many languages.

Reading his introductions to the medical books and some of the letters associated with them may be irritating to the modern reader because of the praise and compliments Maimonides showered over the sultans or officials. It is important to understand though that this was not servility, but a matter of language. The Arabic language and style of the time were rich, colorful and full of nuances. A well-educated, polite man used every flowery phrase to embellish his writing. Maimonides' contemporaries never considered the language he used as fawning. On the contrary, the noble recipient very likely admired Maimonides for being able to use the language so perfectly, poetically and expressively. This custom went hand-in-hand with the appreciation of poetry.

The nephew of Saladin, Al Malik al Mutsaffar, sultan of Hamat, Syria, requested the first medical treatise in 1190. While the subject matter is treated seriously and respectfully, it is obvious that Maimonides needed all his sense of humor to aid him with the task.

To really appreciate how bizarre the situation was, one must remember that Maimonides considered himself an aging man when he reached the age of forty-five, though most people who knew him disagreed with his aged perception of himself. Ten years later, at the age of fifty-five, he saw himself as a *really* old man. In addition, he was a rabbi, the nagid of all the Jews, a man of great dignity and a proponent of a conservative and regulated lifestyle. Yet there he sat at his new task, calmly writing a piece of pornography by the name of *The Treatise on Cohabitation* for a playboy of a sultan who refused to give up his "multitude of young maidens" despite an exaggerated thinness that almost reached a state of emaciation, and severe weakness. Maimonides explained the reasons for the existence of the book in the first chapter.

Apparently, Maimonides begged the sultan to stop his sexual activity, at least for a while; he felt sex was killing the Sultan. Later, in his book, *Regimen of Health*, we can see how he formed this opinion. He claimed that men do not use sex for the purpose of health, or for the sake of procreation, but entirely for pleasure; they go on until they are fatigued, at any opportunity. Sex, he claimed, is detrimental to all men except for those whose temperament is such that a little does them no harm. But men differ only in the degree of harm they do to themselves. Sex is not dangerous to young men whose temperament is "moist," but it is very harmful to old men, to those whose temperament is "dry," and extremely dangerous to the sick or to convalescents. Some convalescents he knew actually died, Maimonides wrote, when they had sex too early after their illness. In addition, it should be regulated even when not too harmful—it should never be indulged in when a man has just eaten and the food is in the stomach but not yet digested, or when hungry, or when thirsty, or when intoxicated, or after leaving the bath, or following exercise or just before it, or on a day before or after bloodletting.

A most important sentence in this treatise states, "Whoever desires the continuance of health should drive his thoughts from coitus all he can." In the *Treatise on Asthma*, he later allowed that some people cannot avoid sex because they produce so much semen, and those people benefit from sex, as long as they don't have too much of it. Generally, he continued, sex is detrimental to all organs, but particularly to the brain: a man given to excessive sex may suffer from premature lapses of memory and mental debility. Also, avoiding sex leads to freedom from infections, purification of the spirit and acquisition of virtues through continence, modesty and piety.

The sultan strongly disagreed. He truly respected and admired his esteemed friend's medical opinions, but surely Maimonides must understand that a man could not possibly waste all those magnificent young maidens residing in his harem? Of course he could not! The sultan not only flatly refused to reduce his sexual activity, but wanted to increase it as much as possible. His unfortunate impotence, caused by his sickness and weakness and emaciation, were just a temporary condition. Maimonides must help him by creating regimens that were relatively easy to follow. In other words, the sultan asked the rabbi to write a sex manual.

Maimonides complied with the preposterous request, and somehow infused it with dignity. He prepared the required regimens, based on foods and medications that were readily available and easy to follow. He wrote the treatise in a matter-of-fact, clear and concise style, and treated it with the same attention to details he gave his philosophical works. The instructions are graphic, and Maimonides showed tremendous knowledge of the subject. He described what foods to eat, and how to regulate baths, exercise and diet to increase sexual strength. He explained which medications and remedies, both internal and external, could help. In a rather candid paragraph, probably unpleasant to the modern reader, he even describes what type of women would strengthen or weaken a man's sexual potency. The grateful sultan tried the cures with enthusiasm. Since the multitude of maidens did not leave any written records of their lives, we unfortunately do not know the degree of success the manual met.

In 1193 Saladin died. His empire suffered from the disputes among his relatives. El Afdal, the eldest son, now ruled Syria. El Aziz, the younger son who was the governor of Egypt from age fifteen, continued to rule Egypt until his death in 1198. At that point, Al Afdal became regent for El Aziz's minor son, Al Adil. On 1200, Al Adil, as the new sultan reunited the empire. These were years of tribulation, increased by the famine and disease that struck in 1201 when the Nile, on which Egypt's economics so greatly depended, was very low.

El Afdal had been a friend of Maimonides since youth, and Maimonides was concerned for his friends' health as he tended to indulge to excess in all the things Maimonides objected to— food, wine, sex, laziness and luxury. This lifestyle drove him to depression, bad thoughts, constipation and indigestion. On his request, Maimonides wrote the treatise, *Regimen of Health*.

The book contains four chapters. The first deals with proper diet, the second discusses diet, hygiene and medications when a physician is not present, the third looks at mental health—probably the first material written about real psychosomatic medicine—and the fourth focuses on prescriptions regarding climate, living conditions, work, bathing, sex, wine, diet and respiratory ailments. The book is incredibly modern in its approach. Maimonides advised the avoidance of immorality and bad thoughts, the governing of passions and mental and physical self-control. Other books followed, though not all survived. Maimonides wrote the *Treatise on Hemorrhoids* for a member of the sultan's family, and it deals with every aspect of etiology and treatment. He had the modern concern for surgery for hemorrhoids, for the same reason physicians are worried about it today—infection and recurrence.

An important work is the *Commentary on the Aphorisms of Hippocrates*. Some scholars censured Maimonides for being less than original in his medical writings, and relying too much on the ancient medical writers. In this book, he showed how wrong they were by freely criticizing Galen and Hippocrates. He studied them and used their teachings, but only as a foundation for his own more scientific system, particularly since he tested each and every remedy he used.

The *Treatise on Asthma* is also amazingly modern. Not only did Maimonides completely understand the nature of the disease and its relation to climate, but the first aphorism in the last chapter describes the effects of pollution and could have come out of a current-day book. He stated that fresh air, clean water and a healthy diet are the foundation of good health of both body and soul. City air, however, he said, is stagnant, turbid and thick because of the big buildings, narrow streets and the refuse of the inhabitants. He suggested that one should reside in a wide-open site that had the living quarters on the upper floor, with lots of sunshine, and the toilets built as far from the living areas as possible. He proposed keeping the air dry and comfortable with drying agents and fumigation and the use of sweet scents.

In 1999, the vizier El Afdil asked Maimonides to write the treatise *Poisons*. The vizier knew how important it was to treat poisons quickly. Many of the necessary ingredients had to be imported because they were not native to Egypt. The vizier imported large quantities and distributed them to the physicians, but many people died before they even reached a doctor. What the vizier wanted was a concise and clear monograph that the patient could read and understand, and then clear the poison using easily available substances.

Maimonides had encyclopedic knowledge of the antidotes and with the extensive literature available on the subject he condensed all the material into a concise and clear book, mentioning many remedies easily obtainable in Egypt. The book was extremely well accepted by the medical community and used for generations; much of the material is still pertinent.

The last medical book Maimonides wrote was the *Discourse on the Explanation of Fits*. Some scholars think it may constitute the fifth chapter of the *Regimen of Health*. Maimonides himself was quite ill at the time, around 1200.

DURING THE NEXT FEW YEARS Maimonides worked very hard, despite growing weakness and many illnesses. The duties of nagid and private physician to the sultan took most of his time, and he could only manage to write responsa, but no more books. He did plan to work on many more books though. He wanted to oversee the translation of all his works into Hebrew, to write a new book about the Aggada, to finish a book he had long ago started on talmudic commentary, another book on the Jerusalem Talmud and finally the book he promised himself to write about his sources for the *Mishneh Torah*. He was only sixty-nine years old, and such plans were not far-fetched. To our loss, this did not come to pass. The years of tragedy, illness and obsessive overwork took their cruel toll. He struggled on until he could no longer continue.

The last few weeks were quiet. The little strength left in Maimonides' once-powerful body slowly dissipated. He took to his bed, too tired to move about, and the constant, nagging pain drained him. Maimonides knew the end was near, but experienced no fear; he was ready to cross the threshold to the next stage. He never wavered in his deep belief in the immortality of the soul and expected the joy of finally really knowing God—the highest virtue he aspired to all his life. He expected to join with God not as a mere spark of light, as he believed the newborn soul must be, but as a complete and mature soul, bringing the knowledge he acquired in life as a tribute to God who granted him this life. He kept thinking about the line he once wrote, that the knowledge of God was like a kiss. According to legends, the biblical Moses, his brother Aaron and his sister Miriam, all died when God kissed them.

The family knew his final request—he wished to be buried in Tiberias, a little town in Palestine, overlooking the lovely lake Kineret. Many other scholars were buried there. There was nothing left to do. Patiently, Maimonides waited for the moment of passing to occur.

Abraham spent much time near his father in those final days. The idea of losing Maimonides devastated him as the loss of Rabbi Maimon had once devastated Maimonides. The sick man could not talk much, but both found some comfort in each other's company. Soon Abraham would assume his father's responsibilities. He would be there for the orphaned nation, perhaps not with the hard, bright flame Maimonides carried within himself, but he would live his life as a steady, wise, reliable leader nonetheless. And Abraham's children would follow in his footsteps, for many generations. Abraham did not even dream about the greatness of his own future, but Maimonides knew. And the thought sustained him during rare moments of sadness.

On the night of December 13, 1204, the large dark eyes closed for the last time. And if the universe is as it should be, then God Himself came to receive the luminous soul that yearned for Him throughout its entire earthly existence.

# ACKNOWLEDGEMENTS

I owe a debt of gratitude to a number of knowledgeable and interested people who kindly helped me in so many ways with this project.

First, to the two people who made the book possible: Barbara Leah Ellis, the editor of the Lives & Legacies series, for suggesting that I write a book on a subject that was so special to me, and for her help, interest and commitment to the project, and Gwendolin Herder, the publisher of Crossroad Publishing, for allowing me to be a part of this fascinating series.

Second, to those who shared their expertise as well as sent me art and photographs to add a visual dimension to the book: Mary Knight, Ph.D., acquisition editor for the American University in Cairo and classical scholar, for sending me her unique reference material and for taking photographs of Cairo/Fustat especially for this book. Gregory Frux, artist, photographer, world traveler and educator, for allowing me to use his personal photographs of Córdoba. Alec Mishori, Ph.D., the noted Israeli art historian, who generously shared his knowledge of medieval Jewish and Islamic art, and allowed me to use his original painting of Maimonides for the book's cover.

Third, to those who helped my research with their knowledge and subject matter expertise: Alan Arbel, for his invaluable historical background research and reference retrieval. Professor

Yael Tsafrir from Tel Aviv University, for obtaining and discussing special Hebrew references I could have never found without her. Professor Avigdor M. Ronn, Ph.D., laser spectroscopy and photodynamic therapy expert, for discussing medieval versus modern medicine with me. Patricia J. Wynne, world-renowned artist of natural history, for reading the material and commenting on Egyptian flora. Joseph Schneider, Esq., lawyer and publishing professional, for his excellent comments on medieval versus modern law. Audra Kemp, legal editor, for reading and commenting on the material as the book developed.

Finally, to the knowledgeable and helpful librarians at the Dorot Jewish Division at the New York Public library, for making their vast Judaica collection so easily and comfortably accessible. They made the research process for this book a true pleasure.

Two points I would like to make about the book. First, the exact dates of many of the events in Maimonides' life are debated. I used the dates most commonly accepted, and when too many opinions differed, those that made sense to me when viewed against the narrative of Maimonides' life. Second, I did not attempt to analyze Maimonides' work as independent of his life — rather, I wanted to show how his complicated circumstances influenced his work. Many excellent books, written by fine scholars, will lead the interested reader into a lifelong study of Maimonides' masterpieces, and the bibliography I provided can be used as a starting point.

# CHRONOLOGY

1135   Moses Maimonides is born on of March 30 (Passover Eve)
His mother dies at birth

1135–1147 (precise dates unknown) Rabbi Maimon remarries
At least three more children are born: David, Miriam and
another sister (name unknown)

1147   Maimon family escapes Córdoba following invasion of
Almohades

1151   Maimon family escapes Almería following advance of
Almohades

1147–1158 (precise dates unknown) While wandering around Spain,
Maimonides writes *Milloth Higgayon*, an introduction to
terminology of logic, based on works of Aristotle; *Maamar
ha-ibbur*, about rules of the Hebrew Calendar; researches
work of the geonim, and collects notes of his father and of
Rabbi Joseph ibn Migash

1158   Maimonides starts the *Siraj* (Commentary on the Mishna)

1159   Maimon family travels to Fez

1160   Rabbi Maimon writes Letter of Consolation

1162   Maimonides writes Epistle on Apostasy

1165   Maimonides arrested by Islamic authorities on grounds of
relapsing into Judaism after (ostensible) conversion to Islam
Maimonides released on Abul Arab ibn Moisha's testimony

Maimon family escapes from Fez to Ceuta, where they board a ship headed to Palestine

Rabbi ibn Shoshan, head of Jewish community of Fez is executed

1165–1166 Maimon family spends a few months in Palestine

1166 Maimon family move to Alexandria; less than a year later, they move to Fustat

1168 The *Siraj* (Commentary on the Mishna) is completed

1170 Maimonides completes *Sefer ha-Mitzvot*; begins working on the *Mishneh Torah*

1172 Maimonides writes the Epistle to Yemen

1174 David Maimonides dies at sea

1175 Marriage between Maimonides and the daughter (name unknown) of Rabbi Mishael Halevi of Fustat

1176–1184 (precise dates unknown) Daughter (name unknown) is born to Maimonides and wife, and dies at young age

1177 Maimonides receives official title of rabbi

1180 The *Mishneh Torah* is completed

1185 Joseph ben Aknin comes to Fustat

1186 Abraham, Maimonides' son is born

1187 Abul Arab ibn Moisha denounces Maimonides as traitor before tribunal

Joseph ben Aknin moves to Aleppo

Maimonides begins writing *The Guide of the Perplexed*

Assumes positions of court physician and nagid

1190 *The Guide of the Perplexed* is completed

Joseph ben Aknin moves to Baghdad

1190–1191 Maimonides writes Epistle on Resurrection

1195 Sages of Lunel in France start corresponding with Maimonides

1204 Samuel ibn Tibbon completes the translation of *The Guide of the Perplexed*

December 13, Moses Maimonides dies

# NOTES

## Chapter 2: Exiles in Thier Own Land

1. *Maor* in Hebrew.

## Chapter 4: Behind the Walls of Fez

1. See "Maimon ben Joseph's Letter of Consolation" in Franz Kobler, *A Treasury of Jewish Letters* (Philadelphia 1954), v.1, p. 168.
2. *Iggeret ha-Shemad* in Hebrew.

## Chapter 5: Eretz Israel

1. Egyptian Jews felt differently. During weddings, a Jewish bride wore men's clothes, and the bridegroom wore women's dresses. This old custom was intended to prevent evil spirits from harming the young couple. When serving as the head of the community, Maimonides objected to the custom as inappropriate and idolatrous, and succeeded in eliminating it.
2. Land of Israel in Hebrew.
3. The 4th when he boarded ship; 10th of Iar, the day of storm.

## Chapter 7: New Beginning in Fustat

1. Also called Misr.
2. Songs that were inserted into the official prayers. Many considered these songs to be inappropriate, and every so often someone attempted to remove them. Later, when a cantor asked Maimonides why he allowed such liberties with official texts, Maimonides answered that while he agreed they were improper, removing them would be worse—it would cause tremendous communal strife.

3. An architectural element that was very popular. It was a room with an open front to the north, elevated between eight to ten feet above ground, surrounded by a low railing and often screened by a wooden lattice.

4. Two other cooling devices were often present—an indoor fountain and an inclined flagstone with water running over it into a basin. With the extensive use of marble, the interior of the houses was cool even in the hottest summer.

5. Some scholars have found evidence leading to the conclusion that David's wife's sister may have been Maimonides' future wife, though there is no absolute proof to that.

## Chapter 10: The Year of Darkness

1. Translated by the author from Igrot ha-Rambam (Letters and Essays of Moses Maimonides), edited by Isaac Shailat, Maaleh Adumim, Israel: Maaliot Press. 1988.

## Chapter 12: The *Mishneh Torah*

1. In Hebrew, the name means "The Second Law." The book was also called *Yad ha-Hazaka*, meaning, in Hebrew, "The Mighty Hand."

2. *Mitzvot* in Hebrew.

3. *Mitzvot Aseh* in Hebrew.

4. *Mitzvot Lo Ta'Aseh* in Hebrew.

5. *Book One: Knowledge.* The articles of faith, the unity of God, His incorporeality, the study of the Law, and the prohibition against idolatry; *Book Two: Adoration.* The percepts that must be observed regularly to show the love for God; *Book Three: Seasons.* The laws concerned with specific times, such as the holidays and the Sabbath; *Book Four: Women.* The marriage laws; *Book Five: Holiness.* Specialized Jewish taboos regarding food and sexual relations; *Book Six: Asseveration.* The laws of vows, which separate one from others; *Book Seven: Seeds.* The laws of agriculture; *Book Eight: Service.* The regulations of the Temple, including worship and community offerings; *Book Nine: Sacrifices.* The laws for offerings, except those of the whole community; *Book Ten: Purity.* The rules of cleanliness and uncleanliness; *Book Eleven: Torts.* Criminal law; *Book Twelve: Acquisitions.* The laws of purchase and sale; *Book Thirteen: Judgements.* Civil law; *Book Fourteen: Judges.* The rights

and duties of magistrates, judges, the Sanhedrin and the king.

6. Translated by the author from Avishur, Yitzhak. *Shivhe ha-Rambam*. Jerusalem: The Magnes Press, The Hebrew University. 1998.

7. Ibid.

## CHAPTER 13: MARRIAGE AND FAMILY

1. Scribes often signed their names as well as that of the person they wrote for.

2. The biblical Patriarch Abraham. Maimonides' admiration for Abraham was second only to his admiration for the biblical Moses, after whom he was named. He once called the Jews "The Community of Moses and Abraham."

3. Translated by the author from *Igrot ha-Rambam* (Letters and Essays of Moses Maimonides), edited by Isaac Shailat, Maaleh Adumim, Israel: Maaliot Press. 1988.

## CHAPTER 14: PHYSICIAN TO THE SULTAN'S COURT

1. This is most likely the situation that inspired so many legends regarding Maimonides' competition with the court physicians.

2. At his time, sympathetic healing was indeed carried to extremes. For example, many doctors believed that feeding of the liver of a mad dog to a man he bit would save the man's life.

3. Translated by the author from Shailat, Isaac. *Igrot ha-Rambam* (Letters and Essays of Moses Maimonides). Maaleh Adumim, Israel: Maaliot Press. 1988.

## CHAPTER 15: THE NAGID

1. The Rabad.

## CHAPTER 16: *THE GUIDE OF THE PERPLEXED*

1. *Moreh Nebuchim* in Hebrew.

## CHAPTER 17: THE ADVERSITY OF FAME

1. A good deed in Hebrew.

2. Translated by the author from Shailat, Isaac. *Igrot ha-Rambam* (Letters and Essays of Moses Maimonides). Maaleh Adumim, Israel: Maaliot Press. 1988.

# BIBLIOGRAPHY

Avishur, Yitzhak. *Shivhe ha-Rambam*, Jerusalem: The Magnes Press, The Hebrew University, 1998.

Benjamin of Tudela. *The Itinerary of Benjamin of Tudela*, California: Joseph Simon/Pangloss Press, 1993.

Dimont, Max I. *Jews, God and History*, New York: New American Library, 1962.

Dubnov, Simon. *History of the Jews*, South Brunswick, NJ: T. Yoseloff, 1967–73.

Elon, Menachem. *Jewish Law (Mishpat Ivri)*, New York: Matthew Bender, 1999.

Even Chen. Jaacov. *Ha-Rambam: R. Mosheh Ben Maimon: Sipur Hayav*, Yerushalaim: Mekhon ha-Ketav, 752 [1991].

Fox, Marvin. *Interpreting Maimonides*, Chicago: The University of Chicago Press, 1990.

Gerber, Jane S. *The Jews of Spain*, New York: The Free Press, 1992.

Goitein, S.D. *Letters of Medieval Jewish Traders*, Princeton, NJ: Princeton University Press, 1974.

———. *A Mediterranean Society: Economic Foundations (Volume I)*, Berkeley and Los Angeles: University of California Press, 1988.

———. *A Mediterranean Society: The Community (Volume II)*, Berkeley and Los Angeles: University of California Press, 1988.

———. *A Mediterranean Society: The Family (Volume III)*, Berkeley and Los Angeles: University of California Press, 1988.

————. *A Mediterranean Society: Daily Life (Volume IV)*, Berkeley and Los Angeles: University of California Press, 1988.

————. *A Mediterranean Society: The Individual (Volume V)*, Berkeley and Los Angeles: University of California Press, 1988.

Grabois, Aryeh. *Medieval Civilization*, New York: Mayflower Books, Inc., 1980.

Graetz, H.H. *History of the Jews*, Philadelphia: Jewish Publication Society of America, 1891–98.

Heschel, Abraham Joshua. *Maimonides*, New York: Farrar, Straus & Giroux, 1982.

Kraemer, Joel L.. *Perspectives on Maimonides, Philosophical and Historical Studies*, Tel Aviv: The Litman Library of Jewish Civilization, 1996.

Maimonides, Moses, edited by Morris Gorlin. *On Sexual Intercourse*, Brooklyn, NY: Rambash Pub. Co., 1961.

————. translated and with an introduction by Shlomo Pines. *The Guide of the Perplexed*, Chicago and London: The University of Chicago Press, 1963.

————. translated and annotated by Fred Rosner. *Treatises on Poisons, Hemorrhoids, Cohabitation: Maimonides' Medical Writings*, Haifa, Israel: Maimonides Research Institute, 1984.

Metzger, Thérèse and Mendel. *Jewish Life in the Middle Ages*, New York: Alpine Fine Arts Collection, 1982.

Minkin, Jacob Samuel. *The World of Moses Maimonides, with Selections from His Writing*s, New York: T. Yoseloff, 1957.

Münz, Isak. *Maimonides: The Story of His Life and His Genius*, Boston: Winchell-Thomas Company, 1935.

Patai, Raphael. *The Children of Noah*, New Jersey: Princeton University Press, 1998.

Rabinowitz, Mordechai Dov, Hirch, Zvi, and Duvkovski, Yosef. *Iggrot ha-Rambam* (Three Epistles and Commentaries), Jerusalem: Mosad Harav Kook, 1967.

Rapel, Dov. *Ha-Rambam ki-mehanekh*, Yerushalayim: Yedi'ot Aharonot: Mikhlelet Lifshits, 758, [1997].

Rosner, Fred, and Kottek, Samuel S. *Moses Maimonides: Physician, Scientist, and Philosopher*. Northvale, New Jersey: Jason Aronson Inc. 1993.

Rosner, Fred. *Sex Ethics in the Writings of Moses Maimonides*. New York: Bloch Pub. Co., 1974.

Schiffman, Lawrence H. *From Text to Tradition*, New Jersey: Ktav Publishing House, Inc., 1991.

Schiffman, Lawrence H. *Text and Traditions*, New Jersey: Ktav Publishing House, Inc., 1998.

Sender, Mae F. *Jewish Time-Travel*, New Jersey: Jason Aronson Inc., 2000.

Shailat, Isaac. *Igrot ha-Rambam* (Letters and Essays of Moses Maimonides), Maaleh Adumim, Israel: Maaliot Press, 1988.

Stitskin, Leon D. *Letters of Maimonides*, New York: Yeshiva University Press, 1977.

Twersky, Isadore. *A Maimonides Reader*, New York: Behrman House, Inc., 1972.

Unterman, Isaac B. *Moses Maimonides: His Life and Teaching*. Miami: Central Agency for Jewish Education, 1978.

Yellin, David and Abrahams, Israel. *Maimonides, His Life and Works*, New York: Heron Press, 1972.

Zeitlin, Solomon. *Maimonides, A Biography*, New York: Bloch Publishing Co., 1955.

# INDEX